THE
VOLVO
TOUR
—— • ——
YEARBOOK
1988

*h*appily the arrival of Volvo as first corporate or 'overall' sponsors of the PGA European Tour has coincided with the performances of European players, individually and collectively, reaching an all-time peak of achievement.

The 1988 Volvo Tour season has been played to a backcloth of Europe holding the Ryder Cup following the historic victory at Muirfield Village in September 1987; Sandy Lyle capturing the US Masters at Augusta in April, and Nick Faldo tieing the US Open at Brookline in June.

Neither of them, however, could claim to be the European number one. Nothing could better illustrate the current strength at international level of PGA European Tour members than Severiano Ballesteros winning the Open Championship at Royal Lytham & St. Annes and securing further Volvo Tour successes to break all sorts of statistical records, firmly stamping his name for the fifth time in 13 years as Europe's leader. Few people will argue that being number one in Europe represents being number one in the golfing world.

What areas of success can the arrival and implementation of the Volvo Tour report? Well for a start, few sporting organisations could embark with the very necessary confidence to make such an all-embracing sponsorship work so efficiently, so soon. The experience and expertise of Tour Enterprises, led by George O'Grady and Gillian Oosterhuis — with a combined 25-year association with tournament golf — has ensured a smooth pathway for our colleagues in Volvo Tour Promotion, who from a standing-start have very quickly formed beneficial relationships with our many valued tournament sponsors and promoters.

The Volvo Tour has brought numerous benefits, quite apart from an 'across the board' assistance to tournament budgets in exchange for Volvo visibility. Volvo Tour courtesy cars for players, media and officials; Volvo Tour practice ranges and player rest lounges have dramatically improved the day-to-day facilities for Tour members, their caddies and immediate families. The aim of these facilities is not simply 'window dressing'. To remain internationally competitive, European players require high incentives and excellent facilities at all our Volvo Tour venues. I feel a very sound starting point has now been achieved.

Volvo, as the Tour's corporate sponsor, is rightly at the centre of golf's continuing prosperity and, with our other major sponsors and promoters, can look forward to an outstanding future in a game where sportsmanship and intensity of competition still walk hand-in-hand.

I wish you happy reading of the inaugural Volvo Tour Yearbook, which chronicles beautifully a season played out in all our main European centres.

KENNETH D. SCHOFIELD

EXECUTIVE DIRECTOR

CONTENTS

LEADER BOARD			
HOLES	PAR	PLAYER	SCORE
72	—20	WOOSNAM	260
72	—17	FALDO	263
72	—14	OLAZABAL	266
72	—14	LYLE	266
72	—14	JAMES	266
72	—13	BRAND JNR	267
72	—12	PARRY	268
72	—11	RIVERO	269

CONTENTS

*Europe's big five at the
Whyte & Mackay Challenge*

A season to savour

BY MICHAEL MCDONNELL

*t*he key question facing Europe at the start of the season after the Ryder Cup success and a series of global personal triumphs was whether such new-found dominance would remain with a handful of top players or manifest itself in a broader confidence that filtered down through the ranks.

In truth, by the end of the year the health of European golf was signalled not just by the great men, most of whom confirmed their class with successive achievements, but also by a wealth of first-time winners and a legion of players – in fact more than ever before – bursting through the £100,000 prize money mark.

Moreover, any suspicion that the newcomers had merely taken advantage of the absence of the top stars to find the side entrance to the winners' circle must be dismissed. In almost all of these first-time triumphs at least one of the established heavyweights had to be beaten in the process.

When this aspect of their triumphs is considered in conjunction with the inescapable fact that Europe's top men – Seve Ballesteros, Sandy Lyle, Nick Faldo, Bernhard Langer and Ian Woosnam – are the best players in the world, then the measure of skill and confidence to beat them – especially for a newcomer – is enormous.

Thus, by the end of the season, it was possible to see the shape of things to come, or rather, the outline of the next generation of players to succeed the present regime that has made such magnificent sporting history. And quite frankly, that was something of a relief because some of the leading players had begun to express concern that there seemed no obvious successors, no thrusting young hopefuls, pushing

hard as the present establishment edged past the 30 year barrier and into golfing middle age.

But once the new talent had emerged – even if some of it had taken time to mature in the cask – the true significance of 1988 also became apparent. On reflection it has been the most complete season in living memory.

Every type of golfer has been rewarded from the superstars and the bright newcomers going places to the honest journeymen who thought perhaps success had passed them by. Not this year. This time, almost everybody took a slice of the cake.

The problem, of course, for observers is to determine some significance in all of this; to determine whether this broad success is more than just the inevitable consequence of bigger and record-breaking prize funds.

It could well be that the all-exempt Tour, criticised by some for its apparent closed-shop policy that prevented anybody breaking in on a week-to-week basis, has had a fundamentally beneficial effect and given the rank-and-file

players the confidence to attack instead of being constantly obsessed with not failing.

None of this applies to the vintage year that Severiano Ballesteros enjoyed as he took the Open title in magnificent style back at Royal Lytham and St Annes where it all began for him in 1979. For a time during the season, it seemed he had only to tee up to become a winner and when the Volvo Tour drew to a close he had scored five victories as well as taking the Westchester Classic title in the United States.

He is a man who seems at peace with himself at last. His business life flourishes and there is more order to his personal life. His prodigious form returned and so too did his warmth. Nowhere was it better demonstrated than during the Suntory World Match-Play when, at a crucial moment, a youngster clicked a camera he had no business to be using anyway as Seve faced a shot. He turned, smiled, posed, then played the shot. . . . and won a million fans.

In terms of historical achievement Sandy Lyle too can rest easy, although he had done most of it before the season was halfway through. He went to the United States to defend his Tournament Players' Championship title and failed to make the halfway cut. Yet such is his erratic style, that this was the precise moment not to write off his chances, particularly as he had already won the Phoenix Open. True enough, he erupted to win the Greater Greensboro title, then a week later became the first Englishman to win the US Masters with a last green putt neither he – nor we – will ever forget.

Nor was Sandy's year one-sided in transatlantic terms because as well as dominating the American money list he returned home to win the Dunhill British Masters and then capture the prize that had eluded him in four previous finals – the Suntory World Match-Play at Wentworth, his home club.

For the beaten finalist Nick Faldo it was a year of paradox. Nobody in the world played more consistently than the former Open Champion in all four majors, yet he emerged with a frustrating collection of second places – eight in all – before gaining his due reward with victory in the Volvo Masters to accompany his win in the Peugeot French Open.

By and large the rest of the establishment ticked over satisfactorily with Ian Woosnam taking time to get started but, once warmed up, clicking into top gear with wins the Volvo PGA Championship, the Carrolls Irish Open and the Panasonic European Open.

Indeed, by the end of the season eight members of the 12-strong victorious Ryder Cup team had emerged as winners to give grounds for confidence as the next match approaches in 1989. Yorkshireman Howard Clark produced a steady display to take the English Open at Royal Birkdale. A more significant aspect of this new tournament is that it fits into a wider framework of 12 national open titles on which the Volvo Tour is to be built.

Jose-Maria Olazabal made it quite clear that the next step in his glittering career must be the capture of a major championship after he won both the Belgian Volvo Open and the German Masters titles. His fellow countryman Jose Rivero took the Monte Carlo Open and even the long-suffering Bernhard Langer emerged from the gloom of his putting troubles to become Epson Grand Prix winner.

Perhaps if there was one moment of impish, but not malicious, delight, it came when the great Seve was beaten on his own course of Royal Pedrena by Mark James for the Peugeot Spanish Open. Then, too, Mark Mouland gave advance warning of what could be the pattern of his career by erupting without warning to peak form to take the Dutch Open.

And yet it was the newcomers who perhaps defined the year and its importance as well as setting personal examples for their other colleagues waiting in the wings to follow. The message was clear enough: there is no monopoly on success. It simply awaits the right amount of self-belief, talent and persistence.

Barry Lane is now established as one of the senior professionals, yet it took

As seen on Tour ...

him seven attempts through the qualifying school before he could safely launch himself. And without question that kind of refusal to give up paid off as he took the Bell's Scottish Open. Similarly for Chris Moody, 13 years on Tour and never higher than 38th in the money list, it was a time of change.

Against one of the strongest fields of the year that included Seve, Nick Faldo, Sandy Lyle and Ian Woosnam, he took the Ebel European Masters Swiss Open at Crans sur Sierre.

His was not the only vintage skill to prevail. Earlier in the year David Llewellyn, 15 years on the Tour, scored his first win (Biarritz Open). Derrick Cooper, 10 years on the Tour and four qualifying schools to his credit, captured the Madrid Open. And there were other breakthroughs too – none so dramatic as that of David Whelan who made the quantam leap from the Condensed Biographies section of the Tour Book and six qualifying schools to beat Nick Faldo in a play-off for the Barcelona Open.

For Australian Mike Harwood (Portugese Open) and New Zealander Frank Nobilo (PLM Open) it was to be the sweet taste of first success and British hearts warmed to the sight of their new hero Peter Baker striding down the fairways of Fulford to become the Benson and Hedges International Open winner.

By the time the book was closed on the year's proceedings almost everybody had gone home happy. The records showed also that international favourites Rodger Davis (Four Stars), Mark McNulty (Cannes Open) and Greg Norman (Italian Open) had all enjoyed a satisfactory season, not least the Irish Dunhill Cup team of Eamonn Darcy, Des Smyth and Ronan Rafferty who confounded the critics and completely outplayed the best golfers in the world to take the Dunhill Cup at St Andrews.

But there was to be a warning note too in all this jubilation and it came from PGA European Tour Executive Director Ken Schofield as he announced the £11.6 million prize fund for 1989.

He declared: 'Our job is to create the opportunity for other players to come forward and join our top men who are now the best in the world. It is vital that they do. And the only contribution we can make is to give them the opportunity. We cannot do more.

'Then, it is up to the Lanes, the Bakers, the Whelans and the rest of the guys who have done it this year, to get back in and do it again.'

Nick Faldo levitates

It was an avuncular observation, not a criticism, even though many of the first-time winners seemed to shoot up from the depths for their moment of glory and then disappear. It was a reminder of their own worth and the fact they are capable of doing it all again.

More to the point, it underlines the old adage that you have to win again to prove the first time was no fluke. Europe's Ryder Cup success emphasised that. The new generation know what task awaits them in 1989.

Bob Torrance gives Ian Woosnam a hand

Double exposure from Paul Way and Peter Baker

Four new winners in 1988: David Whelan, David Llewellyn, Derrick Cooper and Mike Harwood

Eccentric putting style from Bernhard Langer

A smile on the face of the tiger

BY DAVID DAVIES

S everiano Ballesteros: 1988. He won an Open Championship, he won five European events, he won the Westchester Classic in America and, perhaps more to the point, he won his way back into the hearts and minds of golf followers everywhere.

This was the season of sunny, smiling Seve, the greatest golfer of his time, in his pomp. Gone was surly Seve, the whingeing, whining Seve of recent years. Instead there was an almost carefree young man who went about his business as if it were the pleasure it should be.

It was arguably his greatest season. To his power, precision and flair was added not just the new attitude but a new putting stroke and for him that was the all-pervading factor. He undoubtedly made some deep psychological decisions at the start of the season, determining to enjoy his life more, but when, towards the end of the year, he was asked to explain all the smiles against all the previous surliness, he was quite explicit.

'When you play golf at the level I do, it is not just a matter of hitting good — shots. I hit a lot of good shots, so many that it is necessary sometimes to work hard at being humble, for you must be humble in this game. But it is only when you turn those good shots into good rounds that you can have fun and you can only do that by holing putts. When you hole putts, this game is a lot of fun.'

As far as golfing greats go, fun — as previously defined by Jack Nicklaus — consists of there being three holes to play in a major championship and needing a birdie to ensure victory. Fun, therefore, is what Ballesteros had in the Open Championship, although it is ironic that putting, for once, did not

come into it. Earlier in the season the Ballesteros brothers, Severiano and Vicente, had got together on the putting green at Pedrena and decided on a new routine for the former over the ball. Having decided on the line and the strength of the putt, Seve would take his stance and almost immediately hit the ball. It was spectacularly successful and had got Ballesteros, S. into a winning position at Royal Lytham St Anne's by the time he stood on the 16th tee. Nick Price, his only challenger, had played the round of his life but Ballesteros, who had started two behind, was now six under par and level with the man who would not go away.

The 16th, of course, is the hole Ballesteros made famous in 1979 when he hit his tee shot into a temporary car park, got a free drop, hit a wedge to 20 feet and holed the birdie putt. This time, though, he hit a one iron down the middle and had only a wedge left to the green. 'He hit that second shot with the most perfect swing, considering the circumstances, I've ever seen,' said Price afterwards, and the ball almost went into the hole, finishing a couple of inches away.

That stroke, plus a masterly little chip at the 18th, ensured his first major championship since the Open at St Andrews in 1984 and further ensured that his smile became a permanent fixture.

Seve had started the season as he meant to go on. The first tournament was in Spain, on the Santa Ponsa course in Mallorca, and he won it. He won, furthermore, beating the young pretender, Jose-Maria Olazabal, by a six-stroke margin after being level overnight. It was an assertion of his mastery that was to be repeated frequently throughout the season, although Ballesteros recognised that it would not always be so. 'Sooner or later,' he said afterwards, 'he will beat me, because he has tremendous potential and no weaknesses. But he tries too hard when he plays me. I see it in his eyes.'

The next win for Ballesteros was particularly satisfying insofar as it came in the Westchester Classic, which he had lost in 1987 by driving into the trees at the first extra hole of a play-off. And in 1988? Lo and behold he was in a play-off again. Again he scorned safety and this time almost drove the green. With Greg Norman and Ken Green both in the woods and David Frost in a bunker 60 yards short of the green, the Ballesteros birdie was good enough.

You might think that with success almost overwhelming him, Seve would be good and sure to treasure the clubs that were producing it. Not so. He won the Scandinavian Enterprises Open at Drottningholm by five shots on the last day of July and promptly announced that he was going to auction his clubs for a good cause. The Spaniard had won 10 tournaments and half a million pounds with them.

The next to go was the German

Open, at Frankfurt; another five stroke margin, this time over Gordon Brand Jnr after compiling a total of 263, 21 under par.

Three weeks later there occurred the almost impossible, a humdrum Ballesteros victory. The Trophée Lancôme was a procession. He toyed with the field throughout the four rounds, entered the last day with a six stroke lead over Olazabal, seven over Sandy Lyle, and won, easing up, by four.

For the sake of symmetry it would have been right and proper for Ballesteros to win the inaugural Volvo Masters. Not only was it the final tournament of the season and he had won the first, it was being held, as had the first, in Spain — at Valderrama, Sotogrande — and winning it would give him the chance to win more money out of Europe than the leader of the US Money List would win out of the US. It was Ballesteros himself who had worked this out, for not only does he relish a challenge, he loves beating Americans. He believes he has never been given sufficient credit from that quarter and he has, of course, a running feud with the US Tour Commissioner, Deane Beman.

Those were the spurs to goad him forward for the week but, alas for symmetry, he was not up to it. He looked tired, a little overweight and,

perhaps worst of all, he was content with his season. He knew he had achieved enough. He knew that he would establish a new Volvo Tour stroke average record and he knew that whatever happened on the course he had already earned £50,000 bonus money for being top of the Volvo Order of Merit.

He played reasonably well but when Nick Faldo threw a 68 at him in the final round he could not respond with a 65 as he had when the other Nick, Price, did the same thing at Lytham. He

The man and the moments
of the 1988 Volvo Tour

finished second and was left to contemplate his forthcoming marriage to Carmen Botin, his fiancee of several years.

He had hinted strongly that a marriage was imminent when the Spanish Open was played at his home course of Pedrena, although, like the politicians he spoke in code. This time he was saying that he would like to play a great deal more in America in 1989, and we all knew that he would not do that as a single man. But during the Volvo Masters the Madrid newspapers burst into print naming not just the date, but the place. One of golf's longest running sagas was clearly coming to a close.

Seve, despite his fatigue, had made an exceedingly late charge at the Volvo Masters' title, prospecting a pitch at the 17th, the 71st hole of the tournament, in minute detail. If he could get a birdie he knew the resultant roar would upset Faldo ahead. He hit the shot to just over two feet and then, amazingly, missed the putt.

That was the end of his season in Europe, a season in which he had finally shown the world the fullest flowering of his genius. He came into the press room afterwards for the obligatory conference and answered, as he is so willing to do, the same old questions. It was dark before he was allowed to leave, but the significant thing about Severiano Ballesteros, 1988 version, was that as he strode past the computers, the telephones and the typewriters he was still, as he had been all season, smiling.

The victorious 1987 Ryder Cup Tea

Stepping stones to success

BY ANDREW TOTHAM

When John Jacobs took up the reins of professional tournament golf in Britain and Europe 17 years ago, what he had on his hands was a veritable shambles. There were a mere 15 official tournaments for the whole year, players were left to kick their heels in the vacant weeks. Prize money was little over £200,000 and the Tour was run from antiquated, cramped offices at the Oval. It had the air and the attributes of a run-down, struggling organisation, and that is largely what it was.

The highly-polished, highly-successful, highly-acclaimed world-beating European Tour of the 1980s was but a far-off illusion. Few could have believed that golf this side of the Atlantic could ever be what it is today. Jacobs did though, and he said so with conviction. 'I always knew that European golf would take off the way it has. Even in those early days I could sense it was there, that the European upsurge was just waiting to happen but I didn't believe it would happen so quickly.'

That Jacobs was able to turn the mess around and lay the footings of the flourishing European Tour is beyond question. He did it with authority, rashness and good fortune. He survived the traumas of in-fighting, resistance and attack. He came through. Ken Schofield, present Executive Director of the PGA European Tour, says this of Jacobs' efforts: 'John certainly laid the foundations for all we have today and his great contribution can never be over-estimated. We wouldn't be where we are today without him.'

As he sits in the comfort of his New Forest home, Jacobs nowadays is as forthright as ever as to how he transformed the mish-mash of tournaments in 1971 and moulded them into a

John Jacobs,
architect of the Tour

European Tour by the time he left office five years later.

The story is this. Jacobs, aged 46 in 1971, was approached by a group of senior touring pros and the then secretary of the PGA, John Bywaters, to become Director General of the PGA. It was a job few envied for back then the good old days were anything but. Professional tournament golf was going nowhere. On the back of Tony Jacklin's victories in the Open and US Open the sport had received new attention and increasing numbers were wanting to take up the game. But the new momentum was being lost in the shop window. The showcase of the game – the professional circuit – was in chaos. Tournaments were irregular – here one date, there another year, another date. Prize funds were grossly inadequate. Few players made money, they played anywhere for a pittance. There were European events but no hint of European Tour. There was no planning, no co-ordination and no way forward. The fans, although eager to play, were caught in the lacklustre atmosphere of the British Tour. Quite simply they stayed away from tournaments. TV wasn't interested either.

The problem was that the players who made up the PGA were split in two factions. The bulk, some 2,000 strong, and certainly the majority of its ruling executive were 'old guard' club professionals. But there was another faction – the 100 or so players who wanted tournament golf. Heavily in the minority, they and their interests were being ignored.

The two sides marched to a different drum but it was the Tour players who took the beating. Their hopes and lives were being governed by club pros who had no interest in treating them as a special case, hence the apology of the professional circuit. A major and damaging split seemed inevitable.

Mark McCormack summed it up in his review of the 1971 season, The World of Tournament Golf: 'It needed something like the judgement of Solomon to split the PGA into two separate sections (one for Tour pros the other for the club men). And yet plainly something had to be done. Golf was losing out on a great opportunity and the players knew it. The backdrop was that in all the muddle a group of far-sighted and mainly senior touring pros decided during 1971 that the chaos must end. They needed a Solomon alright, but one with the strength of Goliath.'

After behind-the-scenes talks the senior pros and John Bywaters contacted Jacobs. He was a man with an international reputation as one of the game's top teachers and an executive with a chain of flourishing golf centres. More importantly he had been a tournament player himself in the 1950s and early 1960s and one of the strongest advocates of giving Tour players more say in their own destiny. Along with fellow pros Peter Alliss, Bernard Hunt and Harry Weetman, he had demanded an executive made up equally of Tour players and club pros. 'We just wanted to be in control of our own living' recalls Hunt. 'The club pros were deciding our lives for us which was less than satisfactory, to say the least.' The pleas fell on deaf ears and although the four were elected to the executive, they were so heavily outnumbered that their influence was minimal.

A better teacher than player, Jacobs had quit the Tour in 1963 but when the call came to lead the PGA into a new future he hesitated only briefly. The old fight was still there. The will to right the wrong. 'I knew it would be tough,' he says now, 'but I was enjoying a good life through golf and I felt I owed the game something.'

The Tour players, with nothing to lose, were virtually 100 per cent behind him ready to accept what he said. His only proviso was that he was given carte blanche to drive his fundamental changes into practice. Otherwise he risked interference from the executive committee. John Bywaters gave him that verbal agreement and on October 10, 1971, Jacobs stepped into office. Things were about to change. Says Ken Schofield; 'The Tour pros wanted autonomy and John was the strong man who gave them that. He was the right man at the right time.'

From the start Jacobs took the offensive and sought to regain the initiative for the PGA in its tournament dealings. He set about moulding the tournament players into a saleable product. The first thing was to tell all sponsors that there would, in future, be minimum prize funds of £5,000 – way up on the previous norm of £2,000. By increasing the cash more players could survive on tournaments alone. He cut out many of the pro-ams, so popular for little cash at the time, and his master stroke was in forbidding Tour members to play anywhere else while official tournaments were on. He divided the season up with richer tournaments in the autumn. Sponsors would have to pay up if they wanted one of these dates. By 1972 both ITV and BBC were showing tournament golf. Jacobs could now pull the strings. He could offer sponsors firm dates, with the best players guaranteed and TV slots too.

His trump card was Tony Jacklin. A household name, Jacklin wanted to help the Tour but could earn far more with appearance money in pro-ams or other unofficial events. Jacobs knew he needed Jacklin if the Tour was to prosper and so he brought in a rule – the Jacklin rule – which allowed only winners of major tournaments to be paid appearance money in official Tour tournaments. The Tour had Jacklin.

'The main feature about John and his success in those days,' says Ken Schofield,' was his enormous presence. He was known and when he picked up the phone and said 'This is John Jacobs' people listened.'

Within three months of taking office the new Director-General had virtually doubled the amount of prize money on the Tour – from £226,000 in 1971 to more than £440,000 the following

season. The seed was sown and Jacobs rightly predicted that the Tour would be worth over £1.5 million within five years.

And from the start his attention turned to Europe. He realised that geographically Britain couldn't support a full Tour week in, week out. But the Continent offered new horizons. Britain was on the verge of joining the Common Market and Jacobs could see the future for golf. He insisted that Continental tournaments put up £10,000 prize money if they wanted to count for PGA order of merit points. The tournaments agreed. The extra cash and the PGA points would guarantee them the best players. From a hotch-potch British Tour of only eight or nine tournaments within 12 months Jacobs had a European Tour which ran virtually uninterrupted from May to September. Golf had begun to believe in itself. 'It was so vital that we got Europe involved,' says Jacobs now. 'Without that I think the British Tour could even have died.'

Two successful years continued until John Bywaters, who had shielded Jacobs from much opposition in the early days, died suddenly. What followed was two years of bitter infighting that set the Tour back on its heels. The executive commitee, still wary of Jacobs and perhaps jealous of his success, brought in Colin Snape as Bywaters' successor and gave him a brief that brought him right into conflict with Jacobs. Dallas or Dynasty would have been proud of the acrimonious power struggle that followed. The arguments raged for two years with only golf as the loser until a crunch meeting in 1975 when Jacobs, on the brink of being fired, won the day. With the support of Neil Coles (later to become a valuable players' representative on the European Tour board) and other tournament players, Jacobs got what he wanted – the Tour players to have their own separate organisation but within the PGA umbrella. The PGA Tournament Players' Division was born. Professional golf was now in the hands of the players.

Those two years of acrimony still grieve Jacobs. 'They were not happy days,' he recalls. 'The Tour suffered. Our energies were being channelled into fighting each other. It was all such a waste.'

*Tony Jacklin was
the big fish
Jacobs netted to
boost the Tour*

The fight won, the new PGA European Tour regained momentum and with it safely on its way, Jacobs stepped down in 1976 allowing his right-hand man, Ken Schofield, to carry on the work. He left to further his own career as a top teacher for all through his time at the PGA he had been only a part-timer, carrying on his business interests and his teaching schools in the remaining hours. 'I gave the Tour 80 per cent of my resources from only 40 per cent of my time,' he recalls. 'But given that I don't think anyone could have done more in that time. In the end though I always wanted to get the PGA job done and get back to my own teaching.'

But some of his greatest pleasure comes from seeing where the Tour he helped found has got to today. Major championship winners, world-beaters, Ryder Cup triumphs, a prospering Tour spreading the golf gospel to converts throughout Europe and beyond. He is still adamant he knew it was always going to happen – the only thing he got wrong was the timing. 'I couldn't foresee Seve,' he explains. 'He came from nowhere to boost European golf and lead the way with his exceptional quality. The European boom has happened quicker because of him.'

Jacobs also credits Seve for the rise of other golfers such as Sandy Lyle, Nick Faldo and Bernhard Langer. 'By winning the Masters and the Open he showed the rest of Europe that it could be done and gave the other players the inspiration and the belief to come through.'

Ironically the only thing he doesn't like about the modern game is the huge amounts of money. Strange, considering he did so much to boost prize funds at the start. 'It's now got way out of proportion,' he says.

Jacobs keeps in contact with those at the top of the Tour. 'I hope the time will never come when I can't pick up the phone and ask John his advice,' says Ken Schofield.

It was once said of the man that he could cure a hook in two minutes, and a slice in four. While he took much longer – five years in fact – to straighten out the European Tour, there is no doubting that Europe's heady success today really has stemmed from the Tour that John built.

VICTORY
to the promoter

One does not usually associate Mallorca with championship golf. Like the rest of the Balearic Islands it has been slow to recognise the example of the Costa del Sol and other areas of mainland Spain in using sport, and golf in particular, as a focus for tourism. There are only a handful of courses in Mallorca, Menorca, and Ibiza where tourist pursuits have traditionally been centred on the beaches, bars and discotheques.

However, one statistic can no longer be ignored by the government of these beautiful islands – Spain is Europe's most popular destination for golfers – especially those of Northern Europe, whose courses are either closed or often unplayable in winter.

A belief that their region's future prosperity can be underwritten, and enhanced, by sharing in Europe's golf boom brought together both private and public sectors of the Mallorcan holiday industry. And what better way to launch a campaign targeted on the British, German and Scandinavian golf tourist than to employ Europe's finest practitioner of the game's arts as honorary ambassador. Thus the 1988 Volvo Tour began with the Mallorca Open at Santa Ponsa, and this double first turned out to be an unqualified success.

Ballesteros won the event by a handsome six strokes. His margin of victory over the young Basque Jose-Maria Olazabal was surprising, considering his fellow Spaniard's record third round 64, and Seve's own four putts at the 18th in the opening round. But Ballesteros had arrived on the wings of a successful defence of his Spanish PGA title and, with so much personal prestige at stake, was in no mood to be upstaged.

SEVERIANO BALLESTEROS ORGANISED AND PROMOTED THE FIRST MALLORCA OPEN, AND THEN PROVIDED A PERFECT POST-SCRIPT BY WINNING THE INAUGURAL EVENT OF THE 1988 VOLVO TOUR.

That was evident from the outset as Seve thrilled a large gallery of curious islanders and expatriate British who were particularly interested in the performance of Ian Woosnam. He was among the six members of the European team that achieved the historic Ryder Cup victory at Muirfield Village who were in the field. The Welshman had won more than £1,000,000 during 1987, but was clearly not, in racing parlance, ready for the off. He was having technical problems with new Japanese golf clubs, he had put on weight, and had just learnt from a Harley Street specialist that he was afflicted by spondulitis of the spinal region.

Eight victories in one season is a hard act to follow, and 'Woosie' was at odds with himself more than the course – where the greens were surprisingly quick. He made headlines for the wrong reasons when he signed for a par four at the 17th, having actually taken a birdie three. Under the rules of golf he had to accept the higher figure, and his 77 officially became 78.

Woosnam would have been the 65th qualifier for the final 36 holes with a total of 148, but by adding an extra stroke to his score he brought back into the tournament a further 21 players on 149. The PGA European Tour had to find an additional £4000 prize money. Two closing rounds of 71 saw the Welshman finish joint 38th. Woosnam gracefully retired to make further adjustments to his new clubs.

Meanwhile a former American football quarterback, John Slaughter from Texas, Olazabal and Alicante professional Emilio Rodriguez were making the first day running, all with 68 – four under par for the 7150 yards course.

By the end of the second round a Londoner with a dash of enterprise was at the top of the leader board. In the process of reaching a seven under par 137 Neil Hansen had shot a record 66, despite missing a 12-inch putt on the opening green.

The error served only to strengthen the resolve of the 26-year old newly wed from Hertfordshire who used to be an assistant at Chigwell. It was there that he found his first sponsorship in professional golf by marching into the premises of a builder, a tailor and a car dealer and persuading them to back his ability. A merchant banker now supports Hansen's fairway campaign.

By the close of the third day Ballesteros and Olazabal were locked in a tie for the lead at 11 under, the latter after completing the test in only 64 shots. Olazabal, son of a greenkeeper from San Sebastian, had won twice in Europe in 1986 – the European Masters and Sanyo Open – and was not a threat to be taken lightly. He is perhaps the only young European with the potential to outshine Ballesteros, and almost immediately he had flung down the gauntlet. Seve responded to his young rival's 64 with a 67 of his own, birdieing the last to put himself on level terms for the last lap.

Their exploits together in the Ryder Cup in Ohio were now history. With their nearest challenger three strokes adrift, what lay ahead was a private duel between two Spaniards whose paths are destined to cross many times during the next decade.

It was over almost as soon as it had begun as Ballesteros holed from 25 feet on the first green and was out in 33 to be two strokes ahead. The short 12th was the decisive hole as Seve holed from six feet for a birdie, whereas Jose-Maria missed from half that distance, and then three-putted the 15th to put himself four strokes behind.

Another 67 gave Seve a 16 under par 272, and a tally of one eagle and 21

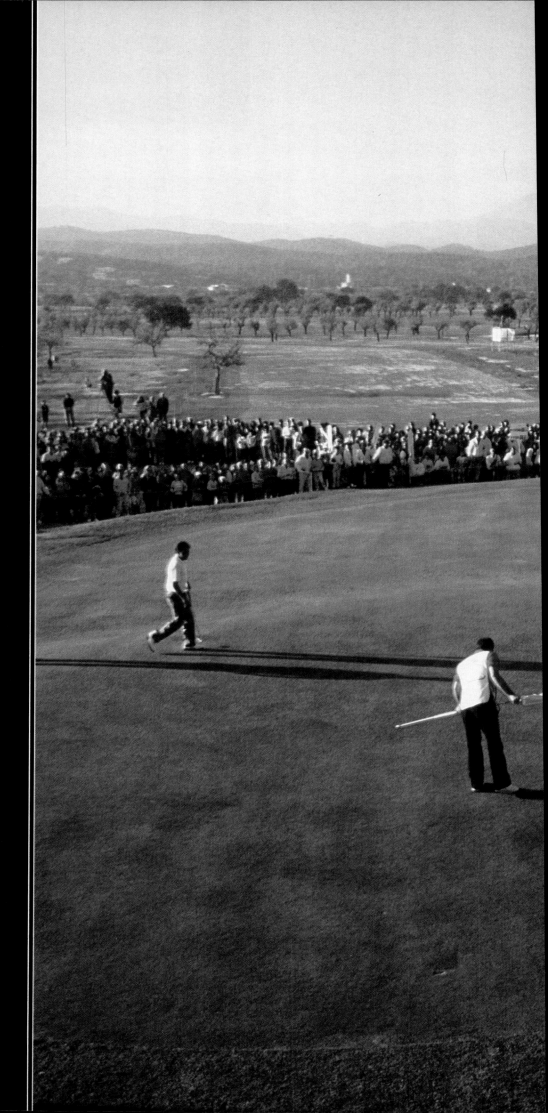

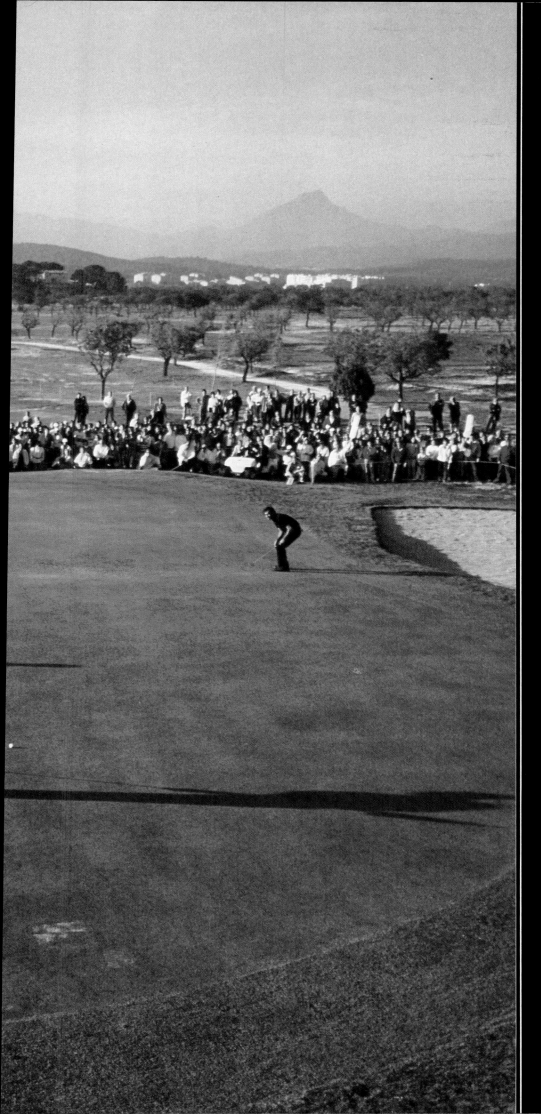

birdies, not including those of the 68 he shot in the pro-am where the Commander of the US Sixth Fleet was given a close-up of his sharpshooting prowess. Olazabal's closing 73 gave him a two stroke margin over Scotland's Gordon Brand Junior whose last day 66 lifted him to third.

Ballesteros paid himself a £33,330 first prize and took his total of victories in Europe to 38 since he turned professional as a 17-year old.

The most promising sign from a British viewpoint was the performance of Barry Lane, whom many judges regard as a future Ryder Cup player. He finished fourth, while Hansen, though subsiding to a last round 79, had the satisfaction of staying ahead of the Ryder Cup trio of Rivero, Darcy and Woosnam, in 15th place.

Ballesteros, however, brooked no argument. From first to last he was in charge and departed to prepare for the US Masters with a job well done.

Balearic panorama for
Ballesteros' penultimate stroke
on the 72nd green

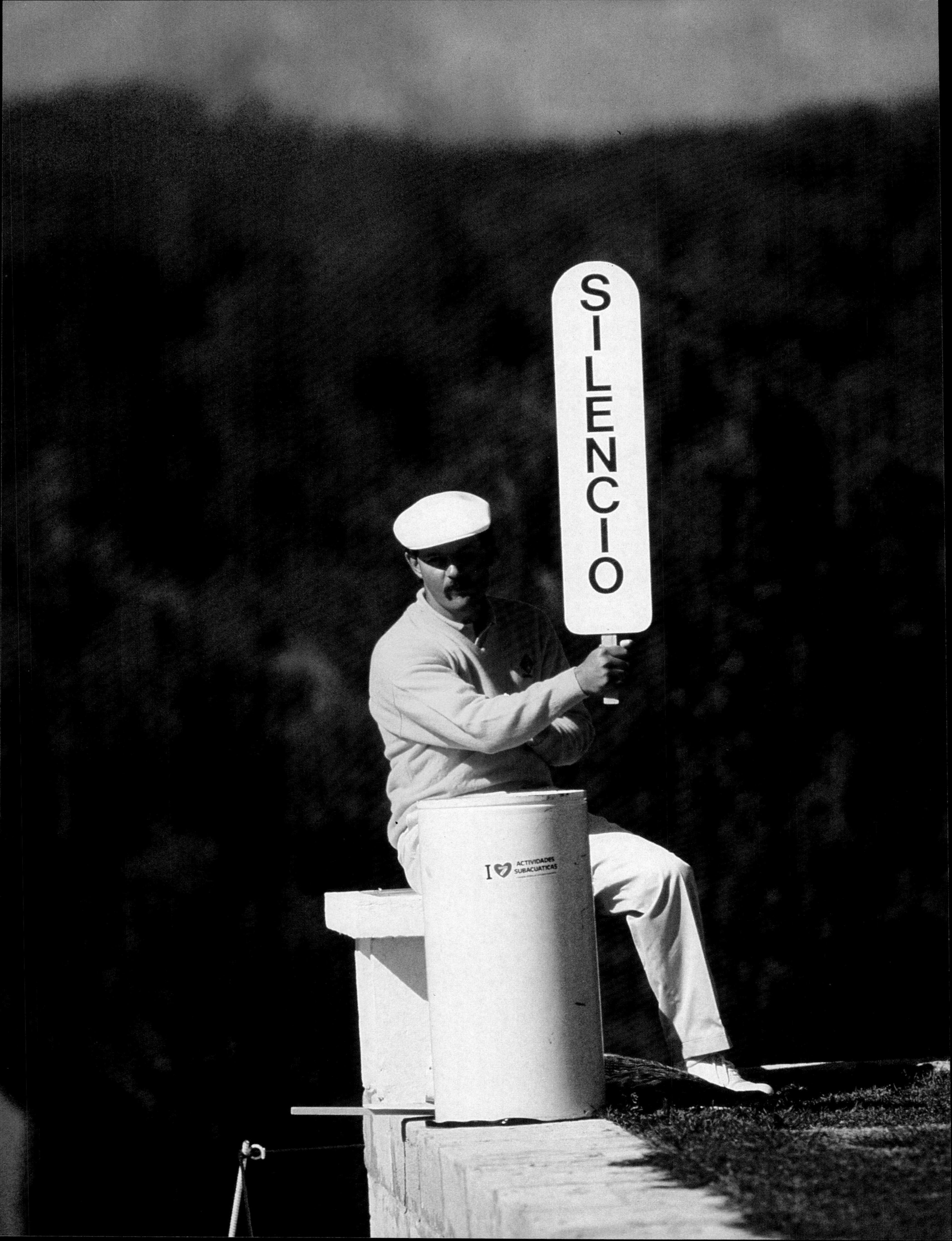
SILENCIO
ACTIVIDADES SUBACUATICAS

Black is back for Ballesteros

*Silencio is golden for Gordon
Brand Junior*

POS	NAME	CTRY	1	2	3	4	TOTAL	PRIZE MONEY
1	Severiano BALLESTEROS	Sp	70	68	67	67	272	£33330
2	Jose-Maria OLAZABAL	Sp	68	73	64	73	278	£22200
3	Gordon BRAND Jr	Scot	76	68	70	66	280	£12520
4	Ronan RAFFERTY	N.Ire	73	70	70	70	283	£8490
	Barry LANE	Eng	71	73	67	72	283	£8490
	Martin POXON	Eng	72	72	69	70	283	£8490
7	John JACOBS	USA	71	73	68	72	284	£6000
8	Des SMYTH	Ire	73	71	72	69	285	£5000
9	Mark JAMES	Eng	73	70	71	72	286	£3646
	Manuel FINERO	Sp	72	71	74	69	286	£3646
	Peter JONES	Aus	72	72	71	71	286	£3646
	Peter BAKER	Eng	71	73	70	72	286	£3646
	John SLAUGHTER	USA	68	72	73	73	286	£3646
	Craig MCCLELLAN	USA	71	73	73	69	286	£3646
15	Juan ANGLADA	Sp	74	75	66	72	287	£2760
	Neil HANSEN	Eng	71	66	71	79	287	£2760
	Andrew MURRAY	Eng	74	72	72	69	287	£2760
	Armando SAAVEDRA	Arg	71	72	73	71	287	£2760
19	Jose RIVERO	Sp	71	71	72	74	288	£2344
	Christy O'CONNOR Jr	Ire	76	71	71	70	288	£2344
	Denis DURNIAN	Eng	76	68	74	70	288	£2344
	David WILLIAMS	Eng	72	73	69	74	288	£2344
	David GILFORD	Eng	75	70	70	73	288	£2344
24	Eamonn DARCY	Ire	74	70	75	70	289	£1840
	David FEHERTY	N.Ire	72	75	72	70	289	£1840
	Antonio GARRIDO	Sp	74	73	70	72	289	£1840
	Brian WAITES	Eng	73	76	69	71	289	£1840
	Jose GERVAS	Sp	75	71	74	69	289	£1840
	Miguel MARTIN	Sp	69	75	76	69	289	£1840
	Richard BOXALL	Eng	72	70	75	72	289	£1840
	Jamie HOWELL	USA	77	71	68	73	289	£1840
	Mats HALLBERG	Swe	76	69	69	75	289	£1840
	Johan RYSTROM	Swe	76	70	73	70	289	£1840
	Jerry HAAS	USA	72	71	70	76	289	£1840
	Calvin PEETE	USA	74	71	71	73	289	£1840
36	Philip WALTON	Ire	76	73	67	74	290	£1500
	Mike MILLER	Scot	74	73	69	74	290	£1500
38	Ross MACFARLANE	Eng	73	73	76	69	291	£1280
	Ian WOOSNAM	Wal	71	78	71	71	291	£1280
	Frederic REGARD	Fr	74	74	72	71	291	£1280
	Emilio RODRIGUEZ	Sp	68	74	77	72	291	£1280
	Mariano APARICIO	Sp	77	72	72	70	291	£1280
	Roger CHAPMAN	Eng	71	73	76	71	291	£1280
	Jerry ANDERSON	Can	73	74	75	69	291	£1280
	Ian YOUNG	Scot	74	72	71	74	291	£1280
	Anders FORSBRAND	Swe	72	72	72	75	291	£1280
47	David J RUSSELL	Eng	76	72	71	73	292	£920
	Eduardo ROMERO	Arg	73	74	72	73	292	£920
	Bryan NORTON	USA	73	70	75	74	292	£920
	Magnus PERSSON	Swe	74	73	74	71	292	£920
	Ross DRUMMOND	Scot	75	73	72	72	292	£920
	Andrew SHERBORNE	Eng	74	75	73	70	292	£920
	Philip PARKIN	Wal	75	73	75	69	292	£920
	Manuel CALERO	Sp	72	74	77	69	292	£920
	Tom SIECKMANN	USA	71	76	73	72	292	£920
56	Greg J TURNER	NZ	71	77	76	69	293	£640
	David LLEWELLYN	Wal	72	75	72	74	293	£640
	Andrew OLDCORN	Eng	75	74	77	67	293	£640
	Michael ALLEN	USA	76	72	74	71	293	£640
	Grant TURNER	Eng	75	74	69	75	293	£640
	John DE FOREST	USA	75	74	72	72	293	£640
62	Carl MASON	Eng	73	73	76	72	294	£464
	Chris MOODY	Eng	71	75	74	74	294	£464
	Peter TERAVAINEN	USA	73	76	72	73	294	£464
	Richard FISH	Eng	76	68	75	75	294	£464
	Emanuele BOLOGNESI	It	77	72	77	68	294	£464
67	Jose Maria CANIZARES	Sp	71	75	73	76	295	£194
	Mark ROE	Eng	74	75	72	74	295	£194
	Malcolm MACKENZIE	Eng	74	73	74	74	295	£194
	Steen TINNING	Den	76	71	74	74	295	£194
	Tony STEVENS	Eng	76	73	74	72	295	£194
72	Mark MOULAND	Wal	73	76	77	70	296	£184
	Andrew CHANDLER	Eng	72	77	72	75	296	£184
	Mark LITTON	Wal	72	74	73	77	296	£184
	Jeremy BENNETT	Eng	76	72	76	72	296	£184
	Jose CABO	Sp	76	73	77	70	296	£184
77	Stephen BENNETT	Eng	76	72	71	78	297	£174
	David RAY	Eng	72	77	72	76	297	£174
	Derrick COOPER	Eng	74	75	74	74	297	£174
	Emmanuel DUSSART	Fr	76	73	75	73	297	£174
	Jose Maria BUENDIA	Sp	73	75	76	73	297	£174
	B Queilpo DE LLANO	Sp	73	75	73	76	297	(AM)
82	Ron COMMANS	USA	72	76	74	76	298	£166
	Steven BOTTOMLEY	Eng	70	75	75	78	298	£166
	Anders SORENSEN	Den	76	73	75	74	298	£166
85	Andres JIMENEZ	Sp	76	73	74	81	304	£162
	Paul MAYO	Wal	76	73	80	75	304	(AM)

Llewellyn shelters with the spoils of victory while Christy O'Connor Junior and Barry Lane join in a champagne celebration

Crowds weren't dampened by the weather

Eamonn Darcy has to branch out with a drop

POS	NAME	CTRY	1	2	3	4	TOTAL	PRIZE MONEY
1	David LLEWELLYN	Wal	64	69	60	65	258	£23691
2	Christy O'CONNOR Jr	Ire	66	66	65	68	265	£15787
3	Barry LANE	Eng	71	65	63	67	266	£8002
	Jose RIVERO	Sp	67	63	69	67	266	£8002
5	Mark JAMES	Eng	67	69	65	66	267	£4705
	Gordon BRAND Jr	Scot	64	69	68	66	267	£4705
	Michael ALLEN	USA	67	66	69	65	267	£4705
	Philip WALTON	Ire	65	66	67	69	267	£4705
9	Simon BISHOP	Eng	64	70	68	66	268	£2771
	Neil HANSEN	Eng	68	66	66	68	268	£2771
	Jim RUTLEDGE	Can	66	67	66	69	268	£2771
	Eamonn DARCY	Ire	63	71	67	67	268	£2771
13	Howard CLARK	Eng	71	64	67	67	269	£2179
	Malcolm MACKENZIE	Eng.	68	68	65	68	269	£2179
	Mike CLAYTON	Aus	67	68	67	67	269	£2179
16	Emanuele BOLOGNESI	It	71	67	68	64	270	£1687
	John MORGAN	Eng	68	69	67	66	270	£1687
	Anders FORSBRAND	Swe	69	69	61	71	270	£1687
	Peter JONES	Aus	70	64	70	66	270	£1687
	Magnus PERSSON	Swe	69	66	67	68	270	£1687
	Ron COMMANS	USA	68	67	67	68	270	£1687
	David WHELAN	Eng	67	68	69	66	270	£1687
	Grant TURNER	Eng	69	69	65	67	270	£1687
	Robert RICHARDSON	SA	69	67	69	65	270	£1687
	Miguel MARTIN	Sp	71	65	71	63	270	£1687
	Jose-Maria OLAZABAL	Sp	67	67	68	68	270	£1687
27	Antonio GARRIDO	Sp	70	66	69	66	271	£1321
	David RAY	Eng	66	67	68	70	271	£1321
	Philip HARRISON	Eng	70	65	70	66	271	£1321
	Roger CHAPMAN	Eng	67	70	66	68	271	£1321
	Santiago LUNA	Sp	66	67	67	71	271	£1321
32	Des SMYTH	Ire	67	70	67	68	272	£1108
	David GILFORD	Eng	69	69	68	66	272	£1108
	Derrick COOPER	Eng	67	66	72	67	272	£1108
	Gery WATINE	Fr	69	68	66	69	272	£1108
	Martin POXON	Eng	69	69	66	68	272	£1108
	Olivier LEGLISE	Fr	68	68	70	66	272	£1108
	Christian BONARDI	Fr	67	69	68	68	272	£1108
39	Bryan NORTON	USA	70	66	66	71	273	£909
	Frank NOBILO	NZ	72	65	67	69	273	£909
	Juan ANGLADA	Sp	70	66	67	70	273	£909
	Gordon J BRAND	Eng	65	68	70	70	273	£909
	Ronan RAFFERTY	N.Ire	68	70	67	68	273	£909
	Jose DAVILA	Sp	69	69	68	67	273	£909
	Chris MOODY	Eng	67	71	68	67	273	£909
46	Tony STEVENS	Eng	71	67	68	68	274	£767
	Magnus SUNESSON	Swe	69	68	69	68	274	£767
	Paul THOMAS	Wal	69	69	67	69	274	£767
49	Johan RYSTROM	Swe	65	68	70	72	275	£710
50	Wayne RILEY	Aus	69	69	67	71	276	£653
	Jeremy BENNETT	Eng	69	68	69	70	276	£653
	Jerry ANDERSON	Can	69	65	71	71	276	£653
53	Emilio RODRIGUEZ	Sp	70	68	69	70	277	£568
	Brian MARCHBANK	Scot	67	70	69	71	277	£568
	Magnus JONSSON	Swe	67	71	70	69	277	£568
56	Thierry ABBAS	Fr	72	66	70	70	278	£511
57	Bill LONGMUIR	Scot	68	70	70	72	280	£483
58	Tim PLANCHIN	Fr	67	70	71	74	282	£454
59	Emmanuel DUSSART	Fr	71	68			139	£313
	Mark MOULAND	Wal	69	70			139	£313
	Carl MASON	Eng	70	69			139	£313
	Peter FOWLER	Aus	69	70			139	£313
	Peter TERAVAINEN	USA	71	68			139	£313
	Anders SORENSEN	Den	67	72			139	£313
	Rick HARTMANN	USA	68	71			139	£313
	Andrew STUBBS	Eng	70	69			139	£313
	Jerry HAAS	USA	72	67			139	£313
	Richard BOXALL	Eng	69	70			139	£313
	Paul CURRY	Eng	69	70			139	£313
	Jean Francois REMESY	Fr	69	70			139	£313

McNULTY

recuperates in style

Mark McNulty had finished runner up to Ian Woosnam on the 1987 European Tour and, with his successes in South Africa, had averaged a victory each month for an entire year. Then this halcyon period was ended by the pneumonia virus, and the 34-year old Johannesburg-based golfer had no option but to rest on his laurels.

His comeback did not commence until the closing weeks of the South African 'sunshine circuit' but, encouraged by no apparent loss of form, he took up his invitation to the US Masters. McNulty finished a creditable 16th behind Sandy Lyle at Augusta, where the defending Cannes Champion Seve Ballesteros was five places further up the merit list. That proximity was not to be repeated at Mougins, where the field assembled agog with Lyle's Augusta exploits.

The Spaniard spoke for all when he declared: 'Sandy's finish was unbelievable. It wasn't luck or a miracle, just perfect play from a great talent. He has not always been given the credit he deserves, but in my mind he has always been a great champion.'

Ballesteros had reached his new base in Monte Carlo after a 25-hour journey during which a combination of thunderstorms in Georgia, flight delays and revised destinations had landed him in Zurich in the early hours. On the way his clubs were 'lost' and he had to borrow a set from local club professional Michel Damiano in order to take part in the pro-am. Then he shot 76 and 78 for a 10 over par 154 to be eliminated after 36 holes for the first time since the Silk Cut Masters of 1983.

The experience perplexed Ballesteros. It was difficult to accept that at the age

MARK MCNULTY ARRIVED ON THE RIVIERA MORE IN HOPE THAN EXPECTATION. HE HAD ONLY JUST COMPLETED HIS RECUPERATION FROM THE DOUBLE PNEUMONIA WHICH HAD FORCED HIM OUT OF GOLF FROM NOVEMBER TO FEBRUARY.

of 31 his body needed more time to cope with jet lag. The previous year he had made the same trip direct from Augusta to win the tournament, beating Ian Woosnam in a play-off. But other factors also had to be taken into account. A golfer of his stature, around whom a tournament has been promoted cannot afford to be eliminated at the halfway stage, simply because he is travel weary.

There is also the not inconsiderable matter of professional pride of performance. The Spaniard is expected to be in title contention wherever and whenever he plays. In the event Ballesteros decided that his days of Atlantic 'hopping' were numbered. He would later change his schedule to avoid the same again.

He took the unprecedented step of apologising to his French golf fans after

taking 41 strokes for the inward half of his second round and hitting the clubhouse with his final tee shot. 'I feel bad about disappointing all those who were planning to spend their weekend watching me' he said. 'It was the worst trip I have had from the US in 14 years. I tried as hard as I could but I could not make the putts that mattered.' And, more revealingly, 'I gave a lot at Augusta last week and there was nothing left for this tournament.'

With Ballesteros consigned to the guillotine, the coast was clear for McNulty to achieve a successful rehabilitation, although it took a closing 66 before his precision golf gave him a three stroke winning margin over imported New Yorker Joey Sindelar.

First there were prominent performances from Australian Wayne Riley, American Ron Commans, Ireland's Philip Walton and the Englishmen Barry Lane and Denis Durnian. Riley led the first round with a four under par 68 containing seven birdies, with Lane a shot behind after holing a 100 yard pitch shot to the 12th for an eagle two. Sindelar (69) was the only other player to break 70, with Ballesteros, reunited with his wayward clubs, languishing 74th equal after his four over par offering. McNulty opened quietly with a regulation 72.

The jockeying for position saw Commans and the Italian Emanuele Bolognesi both shoot 68 in the second round, leaving the American with a three stroke advantage going into the third day. Commans, from Southern California, has proved something of a Riviera specialist recently, being third in Monte Carlo and fourth in Cannes last season. The previous week he had been second in a French tour event

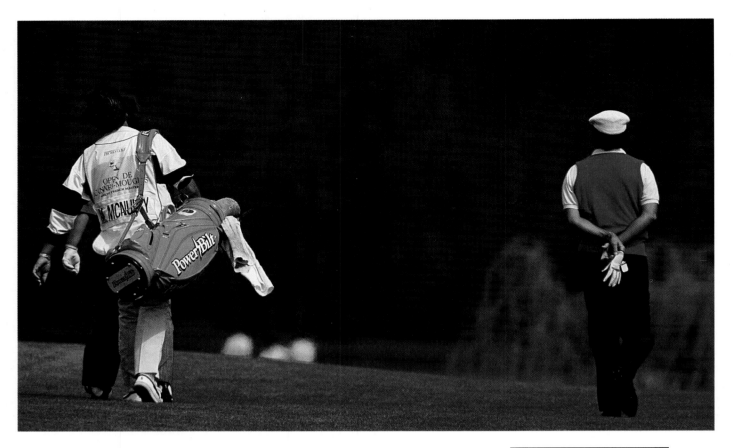

at the Cannes Mandelieu course.

Lane (80) and Riley (75) went smartly into reverse, while the rest of the survivors digested the departure of favourite Ballesteros. Walton, tipped as one of the young men about to make a breakthrough, and the experienced Durnian, had moved among the leaders at the halfway stage. The 26-year old Dubliner made further progress with a third round 68. Sindelar also improved and, having won the Honda Classic and reached sixth place in the US money list of 1988, looked to pose a considerable threat to a home win.

McNulty had other ideas. Having opened with 72–71–70 and scored the first hole-in-one of the tournament season in the process, albeit without reward, he slipped into overdrive for the last lap.

He almost got left on the grid. His opening tee shot was horrendous. He narrowly missed the lake flanking the right of the first fairway and did well to find his ball in thick rough. He escaped with a bogey five, then again with a par at the short second where he was badly bunkered.

Ballesteros drops out after only two rounds

McNulty's troubles are all behind him as he records another victory

However, McNulty played the next 16 holes in seven under par, getting out in 33 to tie for the lead with Commans at six under par. Sindelar holed from 20 feet at the 13th to also move six under, but the Zimbabwe golfer got down from twice that distance on the same green to establish a two stroke cushion. Walton's suspect putting was leading him to a 76 while Sindelar (70) and Commans (72) could make no further progress against the card.

McNulty had only one more alarm, when his first putt at the short 15th pulled up seven feet short. But he sank it and another from the same distance for a birdie at the 16th, and his seventh European victory was secure. His nine under par 279 left Sindelar and Commans sharing second place with Manchester's Durnian next best at 285 after closing with 74 and 70.

'That bout of pneumonia was serious, but it was also a blessing in disguise' said Mark. 'It forced me to take a break from the game, and in future I will pace myself better. I will have to learn to take regular breaks whether or not I have won my last tournament. But it is terribly tempting to carry on.'

American import Joey Sindelar's brave bid for the title came up short

Birdies, eagles, albatrosses and swans

POS	NAME	CTRY	1	2	3	4	TOTAL	PRIZE MONEY
1	Mark MCNULTY	Zim	72	71	70	66	279	£31588
2	Ron COMMANS	USA	70	68	72	72	282	£16453
	Joey SINDELAR	USA	69	74	69	70	282	£16453
4	Denis DURNIAN	Eng	72	69	74	70	285	£9477
5	Tony CHARNLEY	Eng	71	75	74	66	286	£7330
	Jim RUTLEDGE	Can	72	75	71	68	286	£7330
	Howard CLARK	Eng	70	72	73	72	287	£5686
8	Philip WALTON	Ire	71	73	68	76	288	£4065
	Jose-Maria OLAZABAL	Sp	74	69	72	73	288	£4065
	Ove SELLBERG	Swe	71	77	70	70	288	£4065
	Juan ANGLADA	Sp	72	74	71	71	288	£4065
12	Wayne RILEY	Aus	68	75	75	71	289	£3156
	Michael ALLEN	USA	71	73	76	69	289	£3156
14	David LLEWELLYN	Wal	75	74	70	71	290	£2843
	Neil HANSEN	Eng	72	73	75	70	290	£2843
16	Manuel PINERO	Sp	75	73	71	72	291	£2382
	Sam TORRANCE	Scot	76	72	72	71	291	£2382
	Mike HARWOOD	Aus	70	77	73	71	291	£2382
	Mike SMITH	USA	75	72	74	70	291	£2382
	Manuel CALERO	Sp	76	72	73	70	291	£2382
	Paul WAY	Eng	76	73	75	67	291	£2382
	Peter FOWLER	Aus	75	75	71	70	291	£2382
23	Andrew MURRAY	Eng	77	72	72	71	292	£1905
	Tony JOHNSTONE	Zim	73	72	73	74	292	£1905
	Ross DRUMMOND	Scot	77	69	76	70	292	£1905
	Frederic REGARD	Fr	78	68	76	70	292	£1905
	Ronan RAFFERTY	N.Ire	74	70	72	76	292	£1905
	Gordon J BRAND	Eng	71	75	72	74	292	£1905
	Miguel MARTIN	Sp	75	74	67	76	292	£1905
	Mark MOULAND	Wal	75	73	74	70	292	£1905
31	Richard BOXALL	Eng	76	69	71	77	293	£1578
	John JACOBS	USA	74	71	75	73	293	£1578
	Eamonn DARCY	Ire	71	74	73	75	293	£1578
	Glenn RALPH	Eng	73	73	75	72	293	£1578
35	Magnus SUNESSON	Swe	73	74	73	74	294	£1364
	Jeff HALL	Eng	75	75	70	74	294	£1364
	Emanuele BOLOGNESI	It	73	68	76	77	294	£1364
	Antonio GARRIDO	Sp	75	74	73	72	294	£1364
	Andrew SHERBORNE	Eng	74	75	73	72	294	£1364
	Luis CARBONETTI	Arg	73	74	73	74	294	£1364
	Barry LANE	Eng	69	80	74	71	294	£1364
42	Wayne WESTNER	SA	76	73	72	74	295	£1156
	Johan RYSTROM	Swe	75	72	75	73	295	£1156
	Derrick COOPER	Eng	72	74	71	78	295	£1156
	Neil COLES	Eng	75	75	73	72	295	£1156
46	Martin POXON	Eng	72	78	73	73	296	£947
	Anders FORSBRAND	Swe	71	75	75	75	296	£947
	David WHELAN	Eng	71	77	69	79	296	£947
	Ian MOSEY	Eng	76	72	77	71	296	£947
	Ronald STELTEN	USA	78	71	75	72	296	£947
	Emmanuel DUSSART	Fr	76	72	75	73	296	£947
	Frederic MARTIN	Fr	75	74	74	73	296	£947
53	Anders SORENSEN	Den	72	76	75	74	297	£777
	Frank NOBILO	NZ	72	78	72	75	297	£777
55	Andrew CHANDLER	Eng	75	72	76	75	298	£648
	Steen TINNING	Den	72	72	78	76	298	£648
	Emilio RODRIGUEZ	Sp	77	73	74	74	298	£648
	Mitch ADCOCK	USA	74	76	73	75	298	£648
	Yvon HOUSSIN	Fr	77	73	76	72	298	£648
60	David GILFORD	Eng	73	77	71	78	299	£549
	Philip HARRISON	Eng	78	71	78	72	299	£549
	Michel BESANCENEY	Fr	74	73	78	74	299	£549
63	Peter TERAVAINEN	USA	77	73	74	76	300	£345
	Jesper PARNEVIK	Swe	72	77	76	75	300	£345
	Rich HARTMANN	USA	75	75	73	77	300	£345
	David RAY	Eng	73	72	72	83	300	£345
	Jean LAMAISON	Fr	77	73	76	74	300	£345
	Benoit DUCOULOMBIER	Fr	75	73	78	74	300	£345
69	Peter BAKER	Eng	72	74	80	75	301	£192
	John DE FOREST	USA	73	73	81	74	301	£192
	Robert RICHARDSON	SA	76	73	80	72	301	£192
	Thomas LEVET	Fr	73	77	81	78	309	(AM)

NO PRACTICE
is perfect for Cooper

ccordingly, he arrived in the Spanish capital late on the eve of the Cepsa Madrid Open, declaring that practice rounds were a waste of time. His first look at the renowned Puerta de Hierro course came when he was called to the tee at lunchtime the next day. A few minutes later he missed a two foot putt and began his first round with a bogey. It was the sort of start that had become almost routine for the 32-year old Lancastrian who, in 16 years of tournament golf, had had only one victory of note – the 1983 Northern Open.

What was not clear at this stage was the extent of the inspiration lesser lights such as Cooper had gained from the first European victories of the two Davids – Whelan in Barcelona and Llewellyn in Biarritz. 'I have always been a reasonable player and Whelan's breakthrough gave hope to everyone like me' said Cooper. 'There is not that much difference between us and the famous names. It's just that I have been a bit negative with the brains in the past. I felt really positive that week.' Cooper then proceeded to confirm this as the year of the underdog when he shrugged off his unpromising start to rout a veritable squadron of Spaniards and lift his first important title.

The £33,330 top prize far exceeded his total haul in any previous season and fully justified his decision to 'stay at home' during the winter, investing instead in further lessons from his mentor Bob Torrance. Cooper worked particularly hard on his sand-wedge play and pitching. Early results were not forthcoming. Cooper did not make the top 30 in any of the first four tournaments. But he sensed something was about to happen after finding that Puerta de

FOR THE MAJORITY OF PROFESSIONAL GOLFERS, PRACTICE MAKES PERFECT. FOR ENGLAND'S DERRICK COOPER IT'S A CHORE HE CAN HAPPILY DO WITHOUT. THAT'S NOT TO SAY HE IS WORKSHY. IT'S JUST THAT HE PREFERS TO GET STRAIGHT DOWN TO BUSINESS.

Hierro favoured good straight hitting – he returned a first day 70.

The week was to end as it began – with eyebrows raised. The Spanish sponsors were unhappy that Ian Woosnam was not defending his title. He had been given a release by Tour officials to play in the Houston Open which clashed with the following week's Portuguese Open at Quinta do Lago. That would not have precluded his presence in Madrid, but it was then learned that the Welshman had also been signed to appear in a Skins game with Greg Norman, against Nicklaus and Trevino in Phoenix on the Monday of the Houston week.

He clearly could not be competing in Madrid on Sunday, and playing in

Arizona the next day. This was the fifth event of the season and last year's European number one had competed in only the first in Mallorca, finishing 38th. However, Severiano Ballesteros was in the line-up, keen to atone after his Cannes catastrophe. Two days of intensive practice at Pedrena had convinced him all was basically sound. The inquest decided that jet-lag was the reason for his temporary demise but Seve announced that it had been necessary 'to put the whole game back together.' Madrid specialist Howard Clark had arrived, armed with a video camera to search for swing faults, while Australian Rodger Davis was making his first European outing of the year.

All were upstaged for the best part of the first three days by two young members of the host club who underlined the growing strength and depth of Spanish golf. Europe is destined to hear much more of 'Nacho' and Yago – rookie professional Jose Ignacio Gervas and amateur international Yago Beamonte. Gervas (23) shot opening rounds of 65 and 69, Beamonte (22) produced an impressive 69 and 66. After 54 holes they were still sharing fourth place.

Ballesteros began well with 69 and 68, missing the chance to catch Gervas at 10 under par by taking four shots to get down from a greenside bunker at the 18th in his second round. Three putts from less than 10 feet had him turning angrily on a journalist who inquired whether he had changed his putter: 'Don't talk as though I can't putt any more' he snapped. 'It's not fair!' The next day he apologised and agreed that his putting was not what it could be. He was not comfortable over the ball. The statistic that Lyle had taken 10 putts

LANGER

sets the pace

EPSON, SPONSOR OF THE GRAND PRIX OF EUROPE MATCH-PLAY CHAMPIONSHIP, IS TRULY ONE OF THE GUARDIANS OF THE GAME, PROVIDING, AS IT DOES, ONE OF THE BIGGER PRIZE FUNDS OF THE YEAR AND A FIELD TO MATCH. THE WEEK AT ST PIERRE IN EARLY MAY IS ONE THAT IS EAGERLY AWAITED.

*W*hat is it that makes match-play such a riveting form of golf? It is no easier to take one's eye off the action at a matchplay event than to leave the room for a moment during an episode of Fawlty Towers or MASH. It's not only that every single match is interesting because one of the players will suffer the taste of defeat and the other the pleasure of success. Rather, it's like a Feydeau farce. Every entrance and exit is timed to perfection so that the play hurtles on unstoppably and there isn't a moment to pause and take stock.

In the five days of the Epson Match-play championship at St Pierre the following are some of the things that happened: Ken Brown and Rodger Davis both holed in one, Brown winning a Volvo and Davis a Porsche; Ken Schofield, boss of the European Tour, was requested by the Spanish Golf Federation to withdraw the South African golfers from the forthcoming Spanish Open at Santander; Schofield refused. Nick Faldo signed a half-million pound, five-year contract with Pringle to design and wear their clothes; Tony Johnstone got up at dawn and practised his putting on every green on the course because he had discovered that in match–play he was entitled to do that; Langer announced that from now on chocolate was out as a mid-round snack and bananas, apples, pears were to be his staple diet between the first and the 18th holes; then he revealed that he had been receiving medical treatment for 10 hours a day in Munich prior to the tournament.

Naturally enough, those with any knowledge of the unpredictability of golf rushed to put their money on the injured West German, whose first victory

in Europe had come eight years earlier on this same course. Langer himself walked around the pretty clubhouse at St Pierre advising his friends to put their money on anybody but him. Since Langer went on to triumph, this only goes to show that it may be as difficult to pick the winner of a matchplay golf event as it is the 2.30 from Sandown Park.

The way it started was the way match-play events are meant to be: the air was thick with the sound of rattling tumbrils as one member of golf's establishment after another was toppled. Jose Rivero, Jose-Maria Olazabal, Eamonn Darcy and Sam Torrance were all knocked out, Darcy, the hero of the Ryder Cup, being beaten by Robert Lee, the star of the nightclub. The

Torrance of 1988 is a shadow of his former self and his defeat by Ian Mosey was less of a surprise than it would have been in any one of the last seven years.

The best players make a powerful argument against match-play on the grounds that over 18 holes no one is fireproof against anyone else. Nick Faldo, the reigning Open champion, would surely add eloquent testimony to the players' view. In three years of trying he has yet to get past his first match.

He may have felt warm inside at the thought of all the money he was going to make from the Pringle contract but that wasn't protection enough against Garrido who bundled him out of the tournament by 2 & 1.

Ian Woosnam burst into life by beating Ken Brown in front of many noisy, patriotic Welsh fans. He thought he could see light at the end of his tunnel of misery. In the next round he discovered it was the light of the oncoming train. Playing poor golf he crashed out against Des Smyth who was hardly a Dead Eye Dick off the tee either.

Though McNulty and Clark looked impressive, no one seemed to take hold of this event by the scruff of its neck and say 'I'm going to win it and if you don't like it then you can come and try and do something about it.' That's the appeal of matchplay. In a matter of minutes a player in an apparently impregnable position can lose a hole or even a match.

In the semis Langer inched past Davis and McNulty defeated Clark. Langer had looked the shakier of the final-ists after a hard-fought victory over Johnstone and a close shave against John Morgan. But you know what they say about injured golfers.

The final was excruciatingly slow. Langer seemed to take an age. One estimate was that he averaged nearly 14 minutes for each hole of his last two matches. He did play well though, going round in a conservative six under par to beat McNulty by 4 & 3. His victory was due, he said later, to yet another putter. Since Langer changes his putters as often as the rest of us change our shirts there was little significance in the fact that it was one of four he had toyed with for a day or so.

If we did but know it Langer and his putters and putting were about to become a major story. Within a month Langer would admit that the yips had begun again. He'd beaten them once, he'd beat them again by demonstrating astonishing willpower, the sort of strength of character that enables him to prepare slowly and deliberately before every shot regardless, seemingly, of the feelings of both his playing partners and the spectators.

But that's another event and another story. For the moment it was time to laud Langer coupled with the fervent wish, that on a golf course, he would get a move on.

The Russells of spring.
David J and David A of that
ilk clash in an early round

Under the spreading chest-
nut tree, Des Smyth pitches

The star of the big screen.
Antonio Garrido plays him-
self on the 18th green

A wedge of sand as McNulty recovers during the final

FIRST ROUND: MAY 5

WINNER	CTRY	LOSER	CTRY	SCORE	PRIZE MONEY
33T Ken BROWN	Scot	Magnus PERSSON	Swe	2 & 1	
Des SMYTH	Ire	Jeff HAWKES	SA	5 & 4	
C. O'CONNOR Jr	Ire	Mark MOULAND	Wal	3 & 2	
Rodger DAVIS	Aus	Paul WAY	Eng	1 Hole	
Denis DURNIAN	Eng	Noel RATCLIFFE	Aus	5 & 3	
Glenn RALPH	Eng	Barry LANE	Eng	1 Hole	
Bill LONGMUIR	Scot	Ove SELLBERG	Swe	at 19th	
Brian MARCHBANK	Scot	Rick HARTMANN	USA	4 & 2	
Tony JOHNSTONE	Zim	Jose RIVERO	Sp	1 Hole	
Anders FORSBRAND	Swe	Bill MALLEY	Usa	3 & 1	
John MORGAN	Eng	Tony CHARNLEY	Eng	3 & 2	First
Gordon J. BRAND	Eng	David LLEWELLYN	Wal	3 & 1	Round
Antonio GARRIDO	Sp	Mark JAMES	Eng	at 19th	Losers won
Carl MASON	Eng	John O'LEARY	Ire	4 & 2	£1,715
Robert LEE	Eng	Eamonn DARCY	Ire	5 & 3	
Howard CLARK	Eng	J-Maria OLAZABAL	Sp	2 Holes	
Mark ROE	Eng	Gavin LEVENSON	SA	3 & 1	
Miguel MARTIN	Sp	Hugh BAIOCCHI	SA	3 & 1	
Philip WALTON	Ire	John BLAND	SA	at 19th	
Peter FOWLER	Aus	J-Maria CANIZARES	Sp	2 & 1	
Ian MOSEY	Eng	Sam TORRANCE	Scot	3 & 2	
David A. RUSSELL	Eng	Ronan RAFFERTY	N.Ire	1 Hole	
David J. RUSSELL	Eng	David FEHERTY	N.Ire	at 20th	
Roger CHAPMAN	Eng	Manuel PINERO	Sp	1 Hole	

SECOND ROUND: MAY 6

WINNER	CTRY	LOSER	CTRY	SCORE	PRIZE MONEY
17T Ian WOOSNAM	Wal	Ken BROWN	Scot	2 & 1	
Des SMITH	Ire	C. O'CONNOR Jr	Ire	at 21st	
Rodger DAVIS	Aus	Denis DURNIAN	Eng	1 Hole	
Glenn RALPH	Eng	Mats LANNER	Swe	1 Hole	
Bernhard LANGER	WG	Bill LONGMUIR	Scot	at 19th	
Tony JOHNSTONE	Zim	Brian MARCHBANK	Scot	at 19th	
John MORGAN	Eng	Anders FORSBRAND	Swe	5 & 3	Second
Gordon J. BRAND	Eng	Gordon BRAND Jr	Scot	2 & 1	Round
Antonio GARRIDO	Sp	Nick FALDO	Eng	2 & 1	Losers won
Carl MASON	Eng	Robert LEE	Eng	2 & 1	£3,000
Howard CLARK	Eng	Mark ROE	Eng	2 & 1	
Miguel MARTIN	Sp	Peter SENIOR	Aus	3 & 2	
M. KURAMOTO	Jap	Philip WALTON	Ire	1 Hole	
Ian MOSEY	Eng	Peter FOWLER	Aus	1 Hole	
David J. RUSSELL	Eng	David A. RUSSELL	Eng	1 Hole	
Mark McNULTY	Zim	Roger CHAPMAN	Eng	3 & 2	

THIRD ROUND

WINNER	CTRY	LOSER	CTRY	SCORE	PRIZE MONEY
9T Des SMYTH	Ire	Ian WOOSNAM	Wal	2 & 1	
Rodger DAVIS	Aus	Glenn RALPH	Eng	4 & 3	
Bernhard LANGER	WG	Tony JOHNSTONE	Zim	2 & 1	Third
John MORGAN	Eng	Gordon J. BRAND	Eng	at 19th	Round
Carl MASON	Eng	Antonio GARRIDO	Sp	at 20th	Losers won
Howard CLARK	Eng	Miguel MARTIN	Sp	4 & 2	£4,750
M. KURAMOTO	Jap	Ian MOSEY	Eng	at 20th	
Mark McNULTY	Zim	David J. RUSSELL	Eng	5 & 4	

QUARTER FINAL

WINNER	CTRY	LOSER	CTRY	SCORE	PRIZE MONEY
5T Rodger DAVIS	Aus	Des SMYTH	Ire	3 & 1	Quarter
Bernhard LANGER	WG	John MORGAN	Eng	1 Hole	Final
Howard CLARK	Eng	Carl MASON	Eng	5 & 4	Losers won
Mark McNULTY	Zim	M. KURAMOTO	Jap	3 & 2	£9,100

SEMI-FINAL

Mark McNULTY	Zim	Howard CLARK	Eng	3 & 2	
Bernhard LANGER	WG	Rodger DAVIS	Aus	1 Hole	

PLAY-OFF FOR 3RD & 4TH PLACES

Rodger DAVIS (£17,190)	Aus	Howard CLARK (£13,750)	Eng	3 & 2	

FINAL

Bernhard LANGER (£50,000)	WG	Mark McNULTY (£30,500)	Zim	4 & 3	

JAMES
spoils the homecoming

f amily squabbles are often painful and usually regretted. But perhaps one a year is necessary, if only to shake everyone out of the sort of smug complacency with which Voltaire invested his Candide.

Such was the case with the Spanish Open in Santander. It should have been a fiesta. Instead the celebrations fell flat as first politics, and then polemics soured the European tour's pilgrimage to Pedrena, the birthplace of its favourite son.

The first indication that 'outside agencies' were at work came some 10 days prior in a telegram from the Spanish Federation to the Tour's Wentworth headquarters. It conveyed the news that South African golfers would not be allowed to play on the home course of Severiano Ballesteros. The exclusion order appeared to have originated at the Spanish Foreign Ministry and Government involvement was indeed confirmed in subsequent exchanges between the Tour administration and the Federation.

This surprise development was clearly connected in some way with the award of the 1992 Olympic Games to Barcelona. In that context official attention had been drawn to South African golfers by a boxer and tennis player from the Republic who had recently competed in Spain with allegedly incorrect travel documents. In the event, the handful of South Africans then in Europe elected to stay away, although they were given substantial moral support by Ballesteros when the tournament field assembled on the Cantabrian coast. 'We are missing some good players because of my Government's ban, and some of them are very good friends of mine' he declared. 'This ban

THE SPANISH OPEN AT PEDRENA WAS MEANT TO BE A CELEBRATION OF THE ACHIEVEMENTS OF SEVERIANO BALLESTEROS, WHO GREW UP ON THE COURSE. BUT MARK JAMES HADN'T READ THE SCRIPT.

will not change the situation in South Africa and I don't see why people should be prevented from following their profession. The South Africans have contributed a lot to the success of the European tour.'

Few were prepared to argue with that or the installation of Ballesteros as championship favourite. Seve had announced himself with practice rounds of 63 and 62, and then in the Pro-Am, with fiancée Carmen Botin as one of his partners, he shot a nine under par 61 — a new course record.

He talked happily of his early years at Pedrena as an urchin caddie, of the day he earned 40 pesetas for his first 'bag' and gave it to his mother. Along with the other village boys the nine-year old Seve used to play on the beach with a cut-down three iron, employing a twig and a piece of paper to represent a flagstick, thrust into a hole in the sand. At 14, when he was officially allowed to play on the course for the first time, Ballesteros won the Club Caddies' Championship by 16 shots.

The 1988 Spanish Open was being staged at Pedrena as much to mark Seve's achievements and standing in European golf as to promote the game and tourism in north-west Spain.

That Ballesteros felt himself under unusually intense pressure was evident from the first morning. An impressive platoon of his Ryder Cup colleagues, including Open champion Nick Faldo and Ian Woosnam, had made the two-hour road journey over the hills from Bilbao and taken the shuttle ferry across the bay to the course on the hill of Pedrena. It was short — a mere 6300 yards — and softer than usual. It was an inviting prospect.

A healthy gallery had eyes only for Seve, but it was Richard Boxall, one of England's best young professionals, who was the first to profit, opening with a career-best 63. Ballesteros took 72, and was not amused — even less so when Mark James, playing with a new set of clubs, also posted a 63, finding almost forgotten pleasure in his putting.

By the close of the second day Boxall had played the inward half in first 29, then 30 strokes, and was 13 under par. The Surrey golfer found it relatively easy to keep his cool. Elsewhere tempers were frayed as the large field averaged five and a half hours to complete the course. Christy O'Connor Junior, marvelling at the skill of its architect, pinpointed one reason. He counted eight tees and greens squeezed into less than an acre on the crest of one hill. Players continually had to wait for colleagues to putt out or tee off before they could continue their own game.

Ballesteros improved to a 67, but after 36 holes was 12 shots off the pace and Faldo, Ken Brown and James, not to mention Boxall, were all well ahead

View of the Pedrena course with the Ballesteros farm house (second from right) in the background

of him. Also irritated by the pace of play, he could contain himself no longer. His comments about the preparation of the course made headlines and the response from Tour officials was equally forthright. One thing was clear – an argument between the Tour and its best player did no credit to either.

Commonsense prevailed and golf again became the main topic as Faldo returned a third round 62, and James added another 63. The former went out in 29, the latter came home in 31. Then Australian Wayne Riley brought in a stunning 61 to match Seve's Pro-Am score. James, on 194, went into the last round with a three shot lead over Faldo and Boxall, with Riley a further two strokes back.

The three Englishmen played together on the Sunday afternoon and James was soon under attack as both his partners birdied the first hole. At the turn his lead was down to one stroke from Faldo at 14 under, with Boxall one further behind. The blind 30 yard chip that James holed for a two at the 10th provided much needed comfort, but

neither of his rivals would concede an inch. Boxall, in contention for a major title for the first time, bravely responded with three birdies in the next four holes, but then missed the green at the short 15th. The mistake left Faldo, then 15 under, and James, at 16 under, to contest the top prize. Both birdied the 16th and 17th so there was still one stroke between them as they stepped onto the last tee.

James half topped his drive but found the fairway. However Faldo hooked deep into trees and then hit an overhanging bough with his intended recovery. He took four shots to reach the green. James, left with a seven-iron approach, had only to hit the target to be sure of victory. He took a par four to Faldo's six and both recorded 68. James' winning total was a handsome 18 under par. He had putted exceptionally well and had proved a good front runner on the last lap.

James commented drily: 'Even a blind pig finds an occasional acorn.' The Spanish found that curious idiom as incomprehensible as the scowl on the face of their beloved Ballesteros.

Mark Roe slices the main brace

POS	NAME	CTRY	1	2	3	4	TOTAL	PRIZE MONEY
1	Mark JAMES	Eng	63	68	63	68	262	£27703
2	Nick FALDO	Eng	68	67	62	68	265	£18456
3	Richard BOXALL	Eng	63	64	70	69	266	£10406
4	Christy O'CONNOR Jr	Ire	67	66	69	66	268	£7677
	Gordon J BRAND	Eng	70	66	64	68	268	£7677
6	Jose-Maria OLAZABAL	Sp	71	66	65	68	270	£4986
	Eamonn DARCY	Ire	71	68	67	64	270	£4986
	Miguel MARTIN	Sp	70	67	65	68	270	£4986
9	David WILLIAMS	Eng	67	66	69	69	271	£3241
	Colin MONTGOMERIE	Scot	69	64	70	68	271	£3241
	Gordon BRAND Jr	Scot	69	68	68	66	271	£3241
	Derrick COOPER	Eng	69	71	63	68	271	£3241
13	Jose CABO	Sp	73	63	68	68	272	£2552
	Bill MALLEY	USA	69	71	64	68	272	£2552
	Wayne RILEY	Aus	71	67	61	73	272	£2552
16	Peter SENIOR	Aus	68	68	71	66	273	£2341
17	Ken Brown	Scot	67	66	69	72	274	£1990
	Jose-Maria CANIZARES	Sp	71	70	66	67	274	£1990
	Mike CLAYTON	Aus	68	65	70	71	274	£1990
	Seve BALLESTEROS	Sp	72	67	67	68	274	£1990
	Peter FOWLER	Aus	68	67	73	66	274	£1990
	Barry LANE	Eng	70	70	69	65	274	£1990
	David GILFORD	Eng	72	64	70	68	274	£1990
	Philip HARRISON	Eng	69	66	70	69	274	£1990
25	Jose RIVERO	Sp	67	70	70	68	275	£1720
	Anders FORSBRAND	Swe	69	68	71	67	275	£1720
27	Mark ROE	Eng	72	68	69	67	276	£1545
	Glenn RALPH	Eng	66	71	69	70	276	£1545
	Stephen BENNETT	Eng	69	65	69	73	276	£1545
	David LLEWELLYN	Wal	69	71	67	69	276	£1545
	Juan QUIROS	Sp	70	69	68	69	276	£1545
32	Antonio GARRIDO	Sp	71	67	70	69	277	£1329
	Armando SAAVEDRA	Arg	69	71	66	71	277	£1329
	Alberto BINAGHI	It	72	67	74	64	277	£1329
	Michel TAPIA	Fr	66	69	74	68	277	£1329
	Mike MILLER	Scot	68	69	66	74	277	£1329
37	Paul THOMAS	Wal	68	68	70	72	278	£1196
	Emilio RODRIGUEZ	Sp	73	66	71	68	278	£1196
	Michael ALLEN	USA	73	67	68	70	278	£1196
40	Mariano APARICIO	Sp	69	72	71	67	279	£1080
	Jose M CARRILES	Sp	69	70	64	76	279	£1080
	Mike HARWOOD	Aus	73	68	72	66	279	£1080
	David RAY	Eng	70	71	71	67	279	£1080
44	David JONES	N.Ire	69	68	72	71	280	£964
	Ross MCFARLANE	Eng	73	68	67	72	280	£964
	Mark DAVIS	Eng	69	71	70	70	280	£964
47	Paul CURRY	Eng	72	66	70	73	281	£864
	Luis CARBONETTI	Arg	70	65	74	72	281	£864
	Miguel JIMENEZ	Sp	69	70	70	72	281	£864
50	Andrew SHERBORNE	Eng	71	70	69	72	282	£664
	Ignacio GERVAS	Sp	71	69	70	72	282	£664
	Ian MOSEY	Eng	69	70	73	70	282	£664
	Mats HALLBERG	Swe	67	69	73	72	282	£664
	Manuel PINERO	Sp	68	70	76	68	282	£664
	Per-Anne BROSTEDT	Swe	72	69	73	68	282	£664
	Jimmy HEGGARTY	N.Ire	72	68	71	71	282	£664
	Teddy WEBBER	Zim	72	69	71	70	282	£664
	David A RUSSELL	Eng	68	73	70	71	282	£664
59	Emanuele BOLOGNESI	It	71	70	68	74	283	£482
	Kyi Hla HAN	Bur	69	72	71	71	283	£482
	Michael FEW	Eng	71	66	78	68	283	£482
	Peter MITCHELL	Eng	68	71	75	69	283	£482
	John SLAUGHTER	USA	69	69	72	73	283	£482
64	Simon TOWNEND	Eng	70	70	71	73	284	£432
65	Yago BEAMONTE	Sp	69	70	74	73	286	(AM)
	Jeff HALL	Eng	71	70	73	72	286	£415
66	Emmanuel DUSSART	Fr	71	68	78	71	288	£199
	Philip PARKIN	Wal	69	70	74	75	288	£199

NORMAN
laps up the field

EXPENSIVELY IMPORTED FOR THE ITALIAN OPEN AT MONTICELLO, GREG NORMAN WAS ABLE TO COMBINE VICTORY ON THE COURSE WITH THE PURCHASE OF FURTHER MOTORING EXOTICA.

*i*t was James Cagney who first proclaimed from the roof tops 'Look Mum, I'm on top of the world!' Greg Norman said it in much the same way when he flew from Florida for the Italian Open at Monticello, near Lake Como. The blond Queenslander, dubbed 'Hollywood' by his fellow professionals when he exploded into the game a decade ago, may not look like Cagney, but he can certainly act the part.

As befits the official world number one, he boarded Concorde to London, in company with wife Laura, and was then transported by private jet to Monte Carlo to take in the motor racing Grand Prix. The aircraft belonged to British driver Nigel Mansell, an old friend and no mean golfer himself, who was competing in the Monaco race. Norman's love of fast cars and life in the fast lane is well documented, and spectating at the Grand Prix fitted perfectly into his programme for the week. Besides, Laura was eagerly anticipating her first taste of high society in the Mediterranean millionaires' playground. Ostensibly the American-based Australian was back in Europe to play golf for the Italian title, but in truth he had his eyes on a much more valuable prize.

The first indication of the impending arrival of the megastar came when a taxi drew up at the Monticello clubhouse, crammed with suitcases and a set of golf clubs. The driver had dutifully followed his hirer's instructions and delivered his cargo from Monte Carlo – at a cost of some £800.

Norman himself was still some 250 miles away, being custom-fitted for the car of his dreams, one of the exotic F40 models, built by Ferrari to mark 40 years

of production at the company's Modena factory. Only 750 have been made, each capable of more than 200 mph. This ultimate driving experience costs around £200,000, and purchasers have to collect the cars in person.

By the time Norman was ready for practice at soggy Monticello his secret was out. In addition to a reported six-figure appearance fee, he had become a privileged Ferrari customer, elevated to the head of the F40 queue, principally because he already had three cars bearing the famous prancing horse emblem in his garage back home in North Palm Beach. The Australian explained that he regarded the acquisition of luxury cars as an investment, much in the way that aristocrats cherish works of art. A thing of beauty can be appreciated in more ways than one. The Rolls Royce he had purchased in Britain was now worth considerably more than he had paid for it and all his Ferraris had gone up in value. This one would do the same, although he

doubted whether he would drive it more than 20 miles a year.

Norman was now eager to get down to the other business on the week's agenda, but he had to spend 24 fruitless hours in his Milan hotel after an overnight storm swamped the golf course. Rain had fallen for most of the previous fortnight and the water table was so high that the entire area resembled a wildfowl sanctuary. Tournament director Andy McFee called off Thursday's play at 6.30 am and set the groundstaff to work on preparing the course for the following day. It took maximum effort and two par fives, the 11th and 14th, had to be reduced to pars three and four respectively due to hopelessly waterlogged fairways, cutting the course by almost 700 yards.

An opening 69, level par for the revised layout, left Norman feeling somewhat short-changed, especially as the first round leader was one of the smallest golfers in the field, the 5ft 5in Billy McColl. The 31-year old Scot went round in 62 – exceptional golf from a player now earning his living by teaching at Utrecht in Holland. McColl had driven down to Italy for a working holiday from his Dutch base but almost failed to make the starting grid. As he was turning into the course he narrowly avoided a high speed collision with one of those Italian motorists who know what their right foot is for.

Two shots behind him was Ireland's David Feherty, fifth the previous year and the 1986 champion in Venice. He had just started when another storm tracked down from the distant Alps and halted play. Three hours later, in the early evening, he was able to hit his second shot onto the first green. Only 11 holes were possible before darkness

*A dry, sunny moment
at Monticello*

*Greg Norman exchanges more than a
few words with his caddy*

*McNulty gets a big hand
from his caddy*

*The ever-expressive
Jeff Hawkes
took sixth place*

*Emilio Rodriguez makes a
clean getaway. Far right:
Simon Bishop takes a casual
attitude*

VOLVO
PGA CHAMPIONSHIP

LEADER BOARD

HOLES	PAR	PLAYER	SCORE
72	-14	WOOSNAM	
71			274
7		ALLESTEROS	
7		AMES	
7		CNULTY	276
7		APMAN	27
7		WKES	
7		ANGER	
72		AND	28

To the victor the spoils.
Woosnam makes friends with
a new addition to his trophy
collection

POS	NAME	CTRY	1	2	3	4	TOTAL	PRIZE MONEY
1	Ian WOOSNAM	Wal	67	70	70	67	274	£50000
2	Seve BALLESTEROS	Sp	67	68	71	70	276	£26040
	Mark JAMES	Eng	68	72	68	68	276	£26040
4	Roger CHAPMAN	Eng	70	71	71	66	278	£13850
	Mark MCNULTY	Zim	67	71	69	71	278	£13850
6	Jeff HAWKES	SA	67	70	70	72	279	£10500
7	John BLAND	SA	72	70	69	69	280	£7740
	Bernhard LANGER	W Ger	67	66	74	73	280	£7740
	Sandy LYLE	Scot	70	76	68	66	280	£7740
10	Nick FALDO	Eng	71	70	71	69	281	£6000
11	Jose-Maria CANIZARES	Sp	69	68	70	75	282	£5340
	Jose-Maria OLAZABAL	Sp	68	66	78	70	282	£5340
13	Stephen BENNETT	Eng	71	71	71	70	283	£4710
	Des SMYTH	Ire	70	70	72	71	283	£4710
15	Howard CLARK	Eng	70	71	71	72	284	£3980
	Eamonn DARCY	Ire	75	70	69	70	284	£3980
	Rodger DAVIS	Aus	68	72	75	69	284	£3980
	Mike MILLER	Scot	66	74	74	70	284	£3980
	Christy O'CONNOR Jnr	Ire	71	70	69	74	284	£3980
	Ronan RAFFERTY	N Ire	68	71	74	71	284	£3980
21	Tommy ARMOUR III	USA	73	70	72	70	285	£3420
	Tony JOHNSTONE	Zim	73	72	71	69	285	£3420
	Emilio RODRIGUEZ	Sp	76	67	74	68	285	£3420
24	Brian MARCHBANK	Scot	70	69	73	74	286	£3060
	Mark MOULAND	Wal	71	73	68	74	286	£3060
	Andrew OLDCORN	Eng	65	73	76	72	286	£3060
	Manuel PINERO	Sp	72	71	70	73	286	£3060
	Peter SENIOR	Aus	74	71	73	68	286	£3060
29	Ian BAKER-FINCH	Aus	72	74	69	72	287	£2700
	John MORGAN	Eng	73	71	75	68	287	£2700
	Magnus PERSSON	Swe	71	68	73	75	287	£2700
32	Richard BOXALL	Eng	73	69	69	77	288	£2430
	Denis DURNIAN	Eng	72	70	75	71	288	£2430
	Miguel MARTIN	Sp	73	73	70	72	288	£2430
	Teddy WEBBER	Zim	70	71	78	69	288	£2430
36	Simon BISHOP	Eng	72	70	74	73	289	£2040
	Neil HANSEN	Eng	73	73	74	69	289	£2040
	Barry LANE	Eng	70	75	72	72	289	£2040
	Ossie MOORE	Aus	70	70	77	72	289	£2040
	Jose RIVERO	Sp	65	78	75	71	289	£2040
	Mark ROE	Eng	70	76	70	73	289	£2040
	Jim RUTLEDGE	Can	73	72	72	72	289	£2040
	Andrew SHERBORNE	Eng	73	73	71	72	289	£2040
	Greg J TURNER	NZ	72	71	74	72	289	£2040
45	Clive TUCKER	Eng	71	74	74	71	290	£1710
	Brian WAITES	Eng	73	72	72	73	290	£1710
47	David JONES	N.Ire	73	70	74	74	291	£1530
	Malcolm MACKENZIE	Eng	76	70	73	72	291	£1530
	Chris MOODY	Eng	67	73	82	69	291	£1530
	Wayne RILEY	Aus	67	69	78	77	291	£1530
51	David FEHERTY	N.Ire	73	66	77	76	292	£1350
	Mats LANNER	Swe	73	67	77	75	292	£1350
53	Jerry ANDERSON	Can	70	72	78	73	293	£1140
	Manuel CALERO	Sp	71	75	79	68	293	£1140
	Ian MOSEY	Eng	68	75	79	71	293	£1140
	Johan RYSTROM	Swe	72	70	73	78	293	£1140
	Bob SHEARER	Aus	74	72	71	76	293	£1140
58	Hugh BAIOCCHI	SA	67	73	79	75	294	£900
	Peter BAKER	Eng	72	74	76	72	294	£900
	Neal BRIGGS	Eng	73	73	76	72	294	£900
	Rick HARTMANN	USA	70	74	76	74	294	£900
	Gerry TAYLOR	Aus	69	71	74	80	294	£900
63	Derrick COOPER	Eng	72	73	77	73	295	£780
	Michael SLATER	Eng	71	72	78	74	295	£780
	David WILLIAMS	Eng	73	71	73	78	295	£780
66	Vijay SINGH	Fij	73	72	73	78	296	£300
67	Philip WALTON	Ire	72	73	79	73	297	£298

LYLE

becomes a double master

*t*he US Masters champion, Sandy Lyle, became the first player to win the premier Masters titles on either side of the Atlantic when he held off the tenacious challenge of Nick Faldo to win the Dunhill Masters at Woburn by two strokes with a 15-under-par aggregate of 273.

Simultaneously, for what it is worth — and, come to think of it, it is rather a lot — he became the first golfer to have won a million dollars in prize money in America and a million pounds in Europe. Lyle, not untypically, was blissfully unaware that his winning of the £41,660 first prize at Woburn broke the million pound barrier, his haul totalling £1,034,088: 'A million pounds? I'd like to see it ...'

Seve Ballesteros was the only player to have passed the million pound mark in Europe but, rather surprisingly, in spite of having two victories in the US Masters among his American Tour wins he had not done the double. Bernhard Langer had accomplished the American half of the equation but not the European.

With a personal Triple Crown also in his sights in that he was the holder of the German Master, Lyle had opened with a six under par 66 to lead at the close of the first day by a stroke from England's largely unhonoured and unsung Tony Charnley. A resident of the Wentworth Estate, Lyle had been hitting shots into the net in his garden and studying the result on video.

Initially at least, the effect of this self-help could be said to be highly encouraging. Not that his great chum, Lee Trevino, who played with him over the first two days, approved of such visual analysis: 'I play entirely by feel, even to the extent of rendering the grips of my clubs fatter or thinner according to temperature and weather and whether

SANDY LYLE ARRIVED AT WOBURN AS THE CURRENT US MASTERS CHAMPION AND BY THE END OF THE WEEK HAD COMPLETED A UNIQUE DOUBLE.

my fingers are likely therefore to feel puffy or the exact opposite.' Many club golfers are accused of doing no more than further ingraining their swing faults when they practise but Trevino, different as always, insisted that 'You can practise bad habits until they work for you. I did.' The difference, though, is that Trevino knows what goes with what, whereas lesser mortals end up with various elements in their swings which are, in Deane Beman's famous phrase, 'mutually exclusive'.

Like Charnley, Lyle was out in a four-under-par 34. He did take three putts from 40 feet at the 12th, but he came from sand to hole a 30-footer at the 14th. Generally speaking, the putting stroke he borrowed in America earlier in the season from Jack Nicklaus, with the right elbow positioned to act as a piston, has continued to stand up well. Thirty-three years of age, Charnley had never won on the European Tour. He and his wife live out of a caravan for much of the circuit but he was by no means on the breadline, having won £47,000 the previous year and a further £14,000 already in 1988. Charnley's wife, Lucienne, caddies for him. Since

she is not only comparatively slender but has a suspect back, she resorts to a trolley. The one player known to Charnley who definitely objects, on the score that trollies are unprofessional in a professional setting, is Canada's Jerry Anderson.

A humorous fate decreed that they should play together. Hell Bunker is probably not a hazard to compare with a female caddie who feels herself scorned and wisely the two men studiously confined their conversation to less explosive issues. Anderson's argument is that a trolley inevitably slows the pace of play. Few, in this day and age, would dare to be so sexist as to suggest that only males should caddie. The objection is to the trolley, not the caddie's gender, but it would seem to be a case of either smaller bags or bigger wives, if you will pardon the wording.

Leaving his driver unemployed save for the 7th hole, Lyle had a second round 68 which left him three strokes clear at the half-way stage of Spain's Jose-Maria Olazabal and Australia's Ossie Moore. Like many another, Lyle hates to see the driver taken out of the game but, in view of the length he hits a one-iron, it made good tactical sense around the tree-girt Duke's Course, where the ground beneath the branches and the foliage was spasmodically covered in quite thick rough. Over the years, Lyle's Ping one-iron had come to be seen by his fellow-professionals as a fifth limb but one noted at Augusta that he had changed the club, albeit still a Ping model: 'I was perhaps even a few yards longer with the old one but this later Ping seems to have a larger sweet spot and is more forgiving.'

Big two in Buckinghamshire.
Faldo and Lyle duel over the
Duke's course

On a day of drenching squalls, which brought a suspension of play shortly before 4 pm — at least four greens were shipping water, the hiatus lasting an hour and five minutes. Lyle donned his rain jacket at the conclusion of his sixth hole. He then went on to play the next three holes in 3, 2, 3 against the card of 4, 3, 4, holing out of a bunker at the seventh and sinking a 60-footer at the short eighth, which caught the hole 'at the pace of Malcolm Marshall'. At the 14th, there was no whiff of a double-bogey in the air after Lyle's one-iron from the tee, which was perfectly placed to open up a flag, positioned to the green's port side.

The trio of Lyle, Lee Trevino and Barry Lane had gone through the match in front. Like so many rank and file golfers who have been waved through, Lyle hurried his second. He did not quite complete the backswing, the left wrist buckled a little, the face of the club closed a touch and the ball ended just a tantalising yard or two on the wrong side of the fence and out of bounds. A six was the outcome.

Those with totals of more than 147 were guillotined, Sam Torrance missing

his third successive cut.

On the third day, when a thunderstorm caused another interruption of over two hours, Nick Faldo made his move with four birdies in six holes from the third en route to a 67. But Lyle, though not fully at ease with his swing, had a 68 to tee up for the final round, four strokes clear of the reigning Open champion. Having surrendered just one stroke to Faldo in the first five holes, Lyle lost two to him at the 464-yards sixth. Faldo, having duck-hooked from the tee, got down in two from a 100 yards for a four whereas Lyle, after a glorious tee shot, found dense, tangled rough at the face of a bunker and he did extremely well to get down in three more.

At the short eighth, Lyle pulled from his quiver the seven-iron with which he had hit that never-to-be-forgotten shot from sand to the last green at Augusta. Once more it answered the call, a superb stroke to within inches of the flag signalling the counter-attack which was to take Lyle to the title. The one-under-par 71 followed five consecutive rounds over Wentworth and Woburn in the 60s which meant that he was a little matter

of 25 under par for his last seven tournament rounds. Oddly enough, it was Lyle's first win in Britain since the 1985 Benson and Hedges.

The crowd for the last day was over 11,000 which constituted a record for any one day of the Dunhill Masters. If that still does not sound all that many, well, Woburn, for all its other attractions, is far from the most accessible of venues.

The magnet, of course, was the latest instalment of the rivalry between Lyle and Faldo. Despite the weather, the improvement in the conditioning of the Duke's Course under Alex Hay as the Woburn managing director, again came in for much favourable comment.

Nevertheless, it is still the Duke's sister course, the Duchess, which gives rise to my favourite Woburn story. Namely, of the journalistic colleague who, having come straight from the course after a round on a hot and humid day, was introduced to a noble lord. 'I am sorry if I'm sweating,' he said, as he proffered his hand, aware too late of how it sounded, 'But I have just come off the Duchess. . . .'

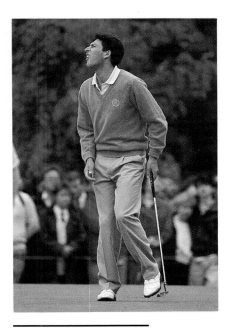

Anguish and effort on the green from Jose-Maria Olazabal, above, and Ossie Moore, below

Champion's salute from Sandy Lyle

POS	NAME	CTRY	1	2	3	4	TOTAL	PRIZE MONEY
1	Sandy LYLE	Scot	66	68	68	71	273	£41660
2	Nick FALDO	Eng	72	67	67	69	275	£21705
	Mark MCNULTY	Zim	69	69	72	65	275	£21705
4	Jose-Maria OLAZABAL	Sp	69	68	71	68	276	£12500
5	Ronan RAFFERTY	N.Ire	72	67	71	69	279	£10600
6	Mark JAMES	Eng	68	75	71	67	281	£8125
	Philip WALTON	Ire	73	68	71	69	281	£8125
8	Jose-Maria CANIZARES	Sp	74	71	69	68	282	£6250
9	Lee TREVINO	USA	69	75	70	69	283	£4875
	Rodger DAVIS	Aus	70	71	70	72	283	£4875
	Ken BROWN	Scot	74	67	74	68	283	£4875
	Bob SHEARER	Aus	70	71	71	71	283	£4875
13	Peter SENIOR	Aus	68	70	72	74	284	£3757
	Christy O'CONNORJr	Ire	73	73	70	68	284	£3757
	Des SMYTH	Ire	70	70	74	70	284	£3757
	Jerry ANDERSON	Can	72	72	72	68	284	£3757
17	Hugh BAIOCCHI	SA	72	70	72	71	285	£3175
	Andrew MURRAY	Eng	70	69	72	74	285	£3175
	Jose RIVERO	Sp	70	71	72	72	285	£3175
	Ian WOOSNAM	Wal	71	73	74	67	285	£3175
21	Wayne RILEY	Aus	72	74	69	71	286	£2887
	Jeff HAWKES	SA	69	71	74	72	286	£2887
23	Eamonn DARCY	Ire	71	70	74	72	287	£2700
	Tony CHARNLEY	Eng	67	73	73	74	287	£2700
	Magnus PERSSON	Swe	73	70	76	68	287	£2700
26	Ossie MOORE	Aus	68	69	75	76	288	£2362
	Neil COLES	Eng	71	71	75	71	288	£2362
	Magnus SUNESSON	Swe	73	69	71	75	288	£2362
	Mats LANNER	Swe	71	76	72	69	288	£2362
	Gordon BRAND Jr	Scot	72	72	73	71	288	£2362
	Robert LEE	Eng	73	71	73	71	288	£2362
32	Manuel PINERO	Sp	70	73	76	70	289	£2050
	Ron COMMANS	USA	74	72	70	73	289	£2050
	Johan RYSTROM	Swe	71	71	72	75	289	£2050
35	Michael ALLEN	USA	74	73	71	72	290	£1725
	Anders FORSBRAND	Swe	73	72	71	74	290	£1725
	Ian BAKER-FINCH	Aus	74	72	71	73	290	£1725
	Ove SELLBERG	Swe	69	75	72	74	290	£1725
	Derrick COOPER	Eng	71	72	77	70	290	£1725
	Barry LANE	Eng	72	70	74	74	290	£1725
	Lyndsay STEPHEN	Aus	72	71	75	72	290	£1725
	Miguel MARTIN	Sp	71	69	76	74	290	£1725
	Bill MALLEY	USA	76	71	70	73	290	£1725
	Malcolm MACKENZIE	Eng	68	75	74	73	290	£1725
45	Frank NOBILO	NZ	74	70	78	69	291	£1325
	Gerry TAYLOR	Aus	69	75	73	74	291	£1325
	Tony JOHNSTONE	Zim	73	72	72	74	291	£1325
	David WILLIAMS	Eng	76	70	74	71	291	£1325
	David FEHERTY	N.Ire	73	74	71	73	291	£1325
	Mike HARWOOD	Aus	74	73	71	73	291	£1325
51	David LLEWELLYN	Wal	74	71	73	74	292	£1125
	Ross MCFARLANE	Eng	71	73	74	74	292	£1125
53	Glenn RALPH	Eng	74	72	75	72	293	£1025
	Roger CHAPMAN	Eng	74	72	73	74	293	£1025
55	John SLAUGHTER	USA	73	72	73	76	294	£875
	Ian YOUNG	Scot	75	69	77	73	294	£875
	David RAY	Eng	71	74	74	75	294	£875
	Manuel CALERO	Sp	73	73	72	76	294	£875
59	Jim RUTLEDGE	Can	72	74	76	73	295	£737
	Antonio GARRIDO	Sp	75	66	75	79	295	£737
	Paul KENT	Eng	72	74	76	73	295	£737
	Andrew OLDCORN	Eng	70	77	74	74	295	£737
63	Howard CLARK	Eng	73	74	70	79	296	£650
	Emmanuel DUSSART	Fr	74	71	78	73	296	£650
	Wayne WESTNER	SA	70	77	74	75	296	£650
66	Chris MOODY	Eng	76	69	71	81	297	£249
	Philip PARKIN	Wal	73	71	79	74	297	£249
68	Vaughan SOMERS	Aus	72	74	76	76	298	£246
69	David J RUSSELL	Eng	72	75	75	78	300	£244

DAVIS
stays behind to win

RODGER DAVIS BYPASSED A WARM UP TOURNAMENT PRIOR TO THE US OPEN AND PROVED IT WAS THE RIGHT DECISION BY TAKING THE TITLE AND THE COURSE RECORD.

*t*he feeling is an all-too-rare one even for the game's superstars. But Rodger Davis had it during his winning of the Wang Four Stars Championship at Moor Park. 'It was as though the ball was on a piece of string to the hole,' the 37-year old Australian said after a second round 63 had broken the composite course record and given him a lead he never relinquished. Nine birdies were almost scant reward for his precision.

And yet Davis had originally intended to be thousands of miles away from the Hertfordshire club. 'I wanted to play in the Westchester Classic to get ready for the Open but the invitation came so late that I decided to stay in Europe and then catch Concorde,' he explained. 'What a good decision that was.' He collected £30,000, almost doubling his Tour earnings for the season at a stroke (or rather 275 strokes). His 13-under par total pushed Eamonn Darcy and Jose-Maria Canizares into a share of second place at 12 under, with Bristol's David Ray a career-best fourth, three shots further back on 279.

The trio refused to let Davis get clean away after his 63. Indeed all three joined the Sydney golfer at the top of the leader board during the third round. Ryder Cup hero Darcy had trailed by three at halfway, but a 69 left him one behind as Davis discovered that even in golf 24 hours is a long time — time enough for someone to cut a piece of string. Canizares and 25-year old Ray also recorded 69s to be two adrift with 18 holes to go.

But Davis managed to keep them all at bay — just. Ray, perhaps as was to be expected, was the first to subside on the

final day, but the Australian's two other closest challengers kept snapping at his heels and it needed a chip and five foot putt at the last — after he had driven into a bunker — for last year's Open runner-up to achieve his first victory for 18 months. Canizares lipped out from 20 feet on the home green and Darcy failed with a 10-footer.

Darcy has twice been denied by players from Down Under in 1988, Mike Harwood having pipped him in the Portuguese Open. But at Moor Park the Irishman really had only himself to blame — poised to draw level when he drove onto the green at the par four 15th, he then three-putted and instead found himself two behind. Surprisingly, defending champion and 'Mr Consistency' Mark McNulty slipped right out of the picture after matching Davis's opening 69, finishing joint 64th. His previous lowest placing in five starts on the circuit was fifth.

Less surprising, sadly, was that Tony Jacklin's first tournament for three years

did not produce a happy ending. He came 102nd out of the 104 starters. The crowds nevertheless flocked to see the former Open Champion's pairing with Lee Trevino on the first two days, but with the weather unkind and exposing his lack of sharpness, he struggled to scores of 80 and 79. Perhaps the unkindest cut was that there was no cut under the pro-am format and, after a more encouraging third round 73, Europe's Ryder Cup captain closed with an 83. It was also, of course, his first appearance since the sudden death of his wife two months earlier. 'Home is the last place I want to be at the moment,' stated Jacklin who, to his credit, did not go back on his promise to play in the Bell's Scottish Open and the Open Championship itself later.

Hugh Baiocchi 'did not go back' either. Only in his case it was to the course on the second day of the Wang Four Stars. Just three strokes off the lead, the South African chose a dramatic way to make a protest about the banning of his compatriots Wayne Westner and Gavin Levenson from the following week's Belgian Open. The pair, who both completed 72 holes at Moor Park, had had their application for visas turned down and Baiocchi commented: 'It was the straw that broke my back and I wanted to stand up and be counted'. His withdrawal was called 'unprofessional' by European Tour committee chairman John O' Leary. 'I have every sympathy with Hugh because we are talking about individual livelihoods being stopped, but I would have liked him to handle the situation slightly differently. I don't think anything has been achieved except to

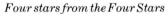

Four stars from the Four Stars   *Michael Allen*

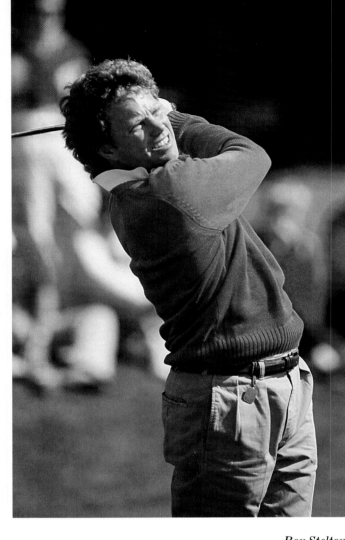

Ron Stelton

cause a problem in this tournament.'

Come Sunday, Baiocchi could still claim a share of victory, however. Comedian Jimmy Tarbuck, one of the event's four celebrity hosts, won the amateur section – and Baiocchi had been his first day partner. Tarbuck will doubtless be back next year to help raise more money for charity. And Ian Woosnam is vowing the same after a tumble playing with his son Daniel had forced him to miss the tournament sponsored by the computer company which backs him.

David Ray

Rodger Davis

OLAZABAL
in the mood for victory

Wounded pride can be a powerful stimulus for any golfer. Add a conviction that just reward has been denied, flavour with a compulsion to reassert a prodigious talent, and you have an explosive cocktail.

Such was the mood of Jose-Maria Olazabal when he entered for the Belgian Volvo Open at Bercuit, some 25 miles south of Brussels. Nine months previously the Spaniard's impromptu samba on the 18th green at Muirfield Village had provided one of the enduring memories of the joyous aftermath of the 1987 European Ryder Cup victory. In partnership with the mighty Ballesteros, the 22-year old Basque had won three matches out of four as the spearhead of the assault on the home invicibility of the United States. He had been one of Tony Jacklin's three personal selections for the team, and the 1986 Rookie of the Year had fully justified the faith that had been placed in him.

Olazabal's contribution to victory had been immense and he clearly harboured thoughts that he had qualified for a privileged passage into major American tournaments. He was not the only European Ryder cup hero to be sadly disappointed. US Masters supremo Hord Hardin had talked disparagingly of 'Scotch Foursomes', and the United States Golf Association remained isolationist in principle.

When the young Spaniard inquired whether he might have merited an invitation or exemption to the US Open at Brookline he was brusquely told he would have to prove his credentials in the qualifying preliminaries. 'Maybe they did not think I was good enough to play in their Open Championship' said

WITH NO INVITATION FORTHCOMING TO COMPETE IN THE US OPEN, JOSE-MARIA OLAZABAL RESPONDED TO THIS SNUB IN THE MOST EMPHATIC WAY POSSIBLE.

Olazabal disconsolately on arrival in Belgium. 'We have beaten them twice in a row and still the Americans do not accept that it is the Europeans who are now playing the best golf.'

It was Eamonn Darcy's first Tour victory for four years the previous season, albeit over 54 holes because of rain, that had clinched his Ryder Cup place in Ohio. Darcy's last green putt to defeat Ben Crenshaw had retained the trophy for Europe but the putter that performed the deed was still missing, and so was the rest of his armoury when the big Irishman began his title defence. Darcy had ditched the clubs which had won him over £60,000 already in 1988 employing instead a new set with fashionable square grooves. He was planning on a 'softly, softly' approach to handling wooded Bercuit where practice had confirmed the greens were on the fiery side.

The golf course was undergoing a metamorphosis, unbeknown to most of the competitors. Officials had decided to soften the greens after complaints in practice that they were too firm. They

were given a double watering, which precipitated further complaints – not because they were soft – but because no warning had been given. The plunging fairways of Bercuit's early holes also had the caddies in a spin. There was talk of special dispensation to use an electric buggy for any caddy who felt unable to cope with the steep gradients. In the event machismo prevailed.

Colin Montgomerie, a Walker Cup player of 1987 who had already begun to make an impression in his debut year, was the first golfer to attract attention as he aced the short second with a five iron tee shot – the first hole-in-one of his career. American Mike Smith set the clubhouse target with a 67.

Olazabal was not long in making his mark. He was out in 31 and by the 12th had recorded seven birdies against the par of 71. The course bit back at the 18th where the Spaniard's hooked drive finished out of bounds in a garden, and he took a double bogey seven. Paul Kent from Bury St Edmunds, who took the last card at the winter School, forced a four-way tie for the first day lead with a matching 67.

For Carl Mason, one of the stalwarts of the British game, the season had so far been unremarkable. He had just been axed three times in a row at the halfway stage, had earned only £400 in the previous month, and domestic bliss was in jeopardy. But wise husbands take their wives' advice and Mason took himself off to consult a sports psychologist. 'My failures were destroying me' he admitted, 'I just wanted to get back to enjoying my golf.' Mason was given an insight into the workings of the mind and declared himself 'unscrambled' after shooting an eagle

Eyeball to ball contact from Gordon J. Brand

and 11 birdies in opening rounds 69 and 68. He went on to finish 10th.

Meanwhile Gordon Brand Junior showed he was in control of his own destiny by producing a course record 66 to share second place behind Olazabal after 36 holes. The Spaniard had twice missed putts of only two feet, but had 69 for a six under par 136. Defending champion Darcy, second the previous week at the Four Stars, had 74 and took an early plane home.

Mike Smith, who was a regular on the US tour before he was forced off by a ruptured disc, was clearly in a productive groove and brought the course record down to 63 in the third round. Olazabal responded with a 64, matching Smith's outward 30 to take a three stroke lead into the final round. He took revenge on the 18th by getting home with two woods and holing from 30 feet for an eagle three and a 13 under par total of 200.

By the time Olazabal, the greenkeeper's son from San Sebastian, had reached the turn for the last time only the margin of his victory was in doubt. He was six shots clear of all rivals and heading for another impromptu celebration at the 18th. Olazabal came home with a 69 for 269 and a four-stroke triumph that was greeted with glee by fellow countrymen Manuel Calero, Nacho Gervas, Santiago Luna, Juan Anglada and Emilio Rodriguez. They showered him with champagne immediately the final putt fell to give 'Ollie' his third European win. Smith held off the twin threat of Yorkshire's Gordon J. Brand and Sweden's Ove Sellberg to secure second place.

The £33,330 top prize took Olazabal to second place in the money list and gave him double satisfaction. 'Now I know I am good enough to beat everyone else' he asserted. On the US Open snub he was, for the time being, keeping his own counsel. 'Let's just say I was in need of this win after 18 months without one' he added. 'It came at just the right time.'

*Aussie aggression from
Wayne Riley*

POS	NAME	CTRY	1	2	3	4	TOTAL	PRIZE MONEY
1	Jose-Maria OLAZABAL	Sp	67	69	64	69	269	£33330
2	Mike SMITH	USA	67	73	63	70	273	£22200
3	Ove SELLBERG	Swe	68	71	70	68	277	£11260
	Gordon J BRAND	Eng	69	70	67	71	277	£11260
5	Peter BAKER	Eng	68	73	67	70	278	£8470
6	Stephen BENNETT	Eng	71	72	69	67	279	£5620
	Eduardo ROMERO	Arg	72	69	71	67	279	£5620
	Ronan RAFFERTY	N. Ire	68	70	69	72	279	£5620
	Tony JOHNSTONE	Zim	69	68	71	71	279	£5620
10	Carl MASON	Eng	69	68	73	70	280	£3840
	Mats LANNER	Swe	73	69	68	70	280	£3840
12	Tommy ARMOUR III	USA	68	72	71	70	281	£3240
	Wayne RILEY	Aus	68	69	71	73	281	£3240
	Gordon BRAND Jr	Scot	71	66	74	70	281	£3240
15	Juan ANGLADA	Sp	68	76	70	68	282	£2880
	Frank NOBILO	NZ	72	68	67	75	282	£2880
17	Neal BRIGGS	Eng	69	72	74	68	283	£2298
	Denis DURNIAN	Eng	70	72	67	74	283	£2298
	Roger CHAPMAN	Eng	69	72	70	72	283	£2298
	Sam TORRANCE	Scot	70	68	71	74	283	£2298
	Ian MOSEY	Eng	71	70	71	71	283	£2298
	Christy O'CONNOR Jr	Ire	71	73	72	67	283	£2298
	Paul KENT	Eng	67	73	69	74	283	£2298
	Anders SORENSEN	Den	68	73	70	72	283	£2298
	Glenn RALPH	Eng	68	72	75	68	283	£2298
	Peter MCWHINNEY	Aus	70	67	70	76	283	£2298
	Brett OGLE	Aus	73	67	72	71	283	£2298
28	Peter MITCHELL	Eng	70	74	69	71	284	£1830
	Anders FORSBRAND	Swe	73	72	72	67	284	£1830
	John MORGAN	Eng	71	72	71	70	284	£1830
	Manuel CALERO	Sp	73	71	70	70	284	£1830
32	Mark DAVIS	Eng	70	71	72	72	285	£1640
	Alberto BINAGHI	It	73	71	72	69	285	£1640
	Mike CLAYTON	Aus	70	68	75	72	285	£1640
35	James SPENCE	Eng	69	70	71	76	286	£1500
	Jamie HOWELL	USA	73	67	71	75	286	£1500
	Ignacio GERVAS	Sp	72	68	72	74	286	£1500
	Brian MARCHBANK	Scot	73	70	73	70	286	£1500
39	Carl STROEMBERG	Swe	69	75	71	72	287	£1360
	Howard CLARK	Eng	72	72	72	71	287	£1360
	Jerry ANDERSON	Can	69	76	71	71	287	£1360
42	Wayne SMITH	Aus	71	73	72	72	288	£1200
	Bill MALLEY	USA	68	69	75	76	288	£1200
	Richard BOXALL	Eng	72	71	75	70	288	£1200
	Tony CHARNLEY	Eng	74	71	72	71	288	£1200
	Martin POXON	Eng	75	68	69	76	288	£1200
47	Ossie MOORE	Aus	71	73	72	73	289	£960
	Andrew OLDCORN	Eng	73	72	71	73	289	£960
	Bryan LEWIS	Scot	71	74	73	71	289	£960
	Bob E SMITH	USA	67	74	70	78	289	£960
	Jeremy BENNETT	Eng	73	70	75	71	289	£960
	Magnus SUNESSON	Swe	71	73	72	73	289	£960
	Mitch ADCOCK	USA	69	71	75	74	289	£960
54	Mark MOULAND	Wal	73	72	74	71	290	£760
	David A RUSSELL	Eng	69	70	77	74	290	£760
	Neil HANSEN	Eng	72	73	74	71	290	£760
57	Bryan NORTON	USA	69	76	73	73	291	£646
	Malcolm MACKENZIE	Eng	70	72	73	76	291	£646
	Stephen MCALLISTER	Scot	69	73	76	73	291	£646
60	Andrew CHANDLER	Eng	68	72	78	74	292	£570
	Jesper PARNEVIK	Swe	69	71	79	73	292	£570
	Colin MONTGOMERIE	Scot	72	71	75	74	292	£570
	Lyndsay STEPHEN	Aus	75	68	71	78	292	£570
64	Philip HINTON	Eng	73	71	78	71	293	£520
65	Armando SAAVEDRA	Arg	71	72	76	76	295	£500
66	Vance WATERS	Eng	72	73	80	80	305	£200

FALDO
bounces back

C hantilly is famous for its lace and porcelain and also as the home of thoroughbred race-horses. Its 18th century Living Horse Museum is a major tourist attraction. It also possesses a majestic golf course.

It was therefore logical to predict that a golfer of complementary calibre would prevail when the Peugeot French Open returned to a venue where the late Sir Henry Cotton, Roberto de Vicenzo and Peter Oosterhuis had been among its former winners.

Expectations were to be fulfilled in the most dramatic fashion when a last hole eagle gave Nick Faldo the championship for the second time, simultaneously ending a sequence of three Spanish victories featuring Severiano Ballesteros and Jose Rivero.

For Faldo it was the perfect cure for a sizeable hangover, engendered by his play-off encounter with Curtis Strange for the US Open title at Brookline. There the Englishman's putting had not matched the quality of his golf from tee to green and after three near-misses in Europe — at Barcelona, Pedrena, and Woburn — he had crossed the Atlantic with a fourth second place on a 1988 record, already remarkable for its consistency. Strange had also made the journey, along with Ballesteros and Sandy Lyle, a formidable if fatigued quartet to contest Europe's oldest Open title outside the Open Championship.

How Faldo triumphed by a short head with a classic finish, worthy of Lester Piggott in his prime, made a fascinating tale. It began with him still concerned with the might-have-beens of his gallant attempt to become the first Briton since Tony Jacklin to hold the Open and US Open titles at the same time. 'I keep thinking about that last putt

FOLLOWING HIS PLAY-OFF DEFEAT IN THE US OPEN, NICK FALDO SHOWED REMARKABLE RECUPERATIVE POWERS AT CHANTILLY.

on the last green at Brookline' he declared prior to the first round. 'I have decided I am going to call it half a Major.'

It was an apt postscript, probably inspired by Strange who had told Faldo not to dwell on his disappointment. 'You also won' said the Virginian before succeeding by four strokes in extra time. Both were understandably still on automatic pilot as they settled into their French routine. Strange had a competent but otherwise unremarkable opening 70. Faldo was equally subdued with a 71, while Ballesteros (72) and Lyle, who included an eight at the eighth in his 76, both lacked their usual sparkle. Most of that came from the man who was to lead for 70 holes, until falling victim to a combination of his own failings and Faldo's flair.

Denis Durnian is one of the characters of the European golf tour. As a merchant seaman he used to hit golf balls off the deck of a freighter into the ocean to keep his game ship-shape. He worked the night shift in an ice-cream factory in Australia to finance his tournament campaign 'down under'. As a club

professional Durnian twice won that championship and four times represented Great Britain and Ireland against the USA clubmen. He lists gardening as his principal hobby — a sardonic reference to a chore he abhors. His wife Rita once bought Denis a garden rake and a book on horticulture as a pointed reminder that he was spending too much time at the golf club!

Durnian's wagon had always been hitched to a wandering star and early in 1987 he decided to quit his club post at Northenden in Manchester. He became a full time tourist at the age of 37 when most professionals are seriously investigating pensionable possibilities. He won nearly £50,000 in the first 12 months back on the circuit he had first joined in 1973, and progress in 1988 had been similarly encouraging with six top 20 finishes prior to Chantilly, where he burst straight to the head of the field with a 65.

Thigh-high rough and pacy greens held no fears for Durnian who had only 25 putts in his opening round — thanks to another of his wife's birthday presents — a putting machine. Durnian uses it most evenings on his hotel bedroom carpet. 'It makes me swing the putter in a straight line' he explained 'and when it works on the course things get silly.'

There were five putts of over 20 feet to laugh about as Denis took a one shot lead over Lincolnshire's Keith Waters and Richard Boxall, who holed a four iron shot of 210 yards for an eagle two at the fifth.

There was also some unscheduled entertainment from Australian Craig Parry. The applause for a perfect opening drive had barely ceased when a particularly chic Parisienne darted from the gallery to purloin his ball from the

middle of the fairway. Recognising he was about to be penalty-stricken the Perth golfer decided this was a 'sheila' who could not be allowed to escape his clutches. He was accorded a thunderous ovation as he snared his quarry with a furious sprint and bear-hug. The maiden surrendered without a fight and was quickly persuaded to replace her ill-gotten gain at the appropriate spot. Parry failed to secure his, as rounds of 73 and 76 left him a victim of the halfway axe.

Sandy Lyle also took an early flight home with a 36-hole total of 150, 17 behind Durnian who added a 68 for seven under par to take a five stroke halfway advantage over Faldo. Ballesteros was back in the pack on 143, lacking inspiration, especially with his putter, and Strange was on the same mark. Boxall and the Australians

Wayne Riley and Peter Senior were the only other players under par, but the principal question was whether Faldo could make up his leeway.

Durnian's lead was down to three shots when he and Faldo reached the 18th in the third round, only for the Manchester golfer to chip in for an eagle three against Faldo's birdie four at the last. Riley, despite an attack of food poisoning, returned 67 to catch Faldo on 206, while Ireland's David Feherty made a charge with a 66 for 208.

Durnian's first major victory looked a formality, especially when he stepped on to the 17th tee in the final round still two shots clear of Faldo and Riley. The former, up ahead, had secured his par four at the 17th and was preparing to drive at the splendid 575-yards closing hole when Durnian snap-hooked to disaster. His two iron approach dived

into a thicket short of the green and after hacking out he then hit a poor chip to take a double bogey six.

Faldo was through the gap in a flash. His second to the last with a three wood zoomed 260 yards to the heart of the green and the eagle landed on his card when he holed a snaking 30-foot putt for a 68 and a six under par 274. It gave him his first victory of the season – by two strokes over the downcast Durnian and Riley, who had par fives at the last, to tie second on 276. History had repeated itself – for five years earlier a last hole eagle at La Boulie had won the French title for Faldo, after a play-off with Jose-Maria Canizares and David J. Russell.

He rightly rejoiced in this second coup. It had been a tour de force, and a timely boost to his morale following his disappointment at Brookline.

Denis Durnian
celebrates a holed
chip shot

Disaster for Durnian
as his caddie
is bush bound

Leftish tendencies
from Wayne Riley

Overwhelmed by
excitement?

Fresh from his US Open victory, Curtis Strange gave best to Faldo in France

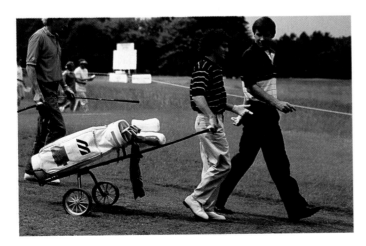

Alain Prost switches to two wheels in partnership with Faldo in the Pro-Am

POS	NAME	CTRY	1	2	3	4	TOTAL	PRIZE MONEY
1	Nick FALDO	Eng	71	67	68	68	274	£47236
2	Denis DURNIAN	Eng	65	68	69	74	276	£24600
	Wayne RILEY	Aus	72	67	67	70	276	£24600
4	Ossie MOORE	Aus	71	69	69	69	278	£13084
	David FEHERTY	N.Ire	72	70	66	70	278	£13084
6	Peter SENIOR	Aus	70	69	68	72	279	£9919
7	Ronan RAFFERTY	N.Ire	73	69	74	64	280	£7794
	David WILLIAMS	Eng	73	67	69	71	280	£7794
9	Malcolm MACKENZIE	Eng	72	70	68	72	282	£5526
	Sam TORRANCE	Scot	69	73	70	70	282	£5526
	Miguel MARTIN	Sp	75	68	65	74	282	£5526
	Anders FORSBRAND	Swe	72	72	67	71	282	£5526
13	Curtis STRANGE	USA	70	73	70	70	283	£4563
14	Roger CHAPMAN	Eng	69	71	74	70	284	£3996
	Seve BALLESTEROS	Sp	72	71	69	72	284	£3996
	Jerry ANDERSON	Can	71	72	71	70	284	£3996
	Paul CURRY	Eng	73	73	71	67	284	£3996
	Andrew MURRAY	Eng	74	67	70	73	284	£3996
19	Peter BAKER	Eng	72	71	71	72	286	£3106
	Philip HARRISON	Eng	71	74	68	73	286	£3106
	John DE FOREST	USA	75	70	70	71	286	£3106
	Jose-Maria OLAZABAL	Sp	74	67	73	72	286	£3106
	Andrew CHANDLER	Eng	73	72	70	71	286	£3106
	Richard BOXALL	Eng	66	73	75	72	286	£3106
	Ken BROWN	Scot	70	72	75	69	286	£3106
	Mark ROE	Eng	69	74	71	72	286	£3106
	Ian MOSEY	Eng	72	71	72	71	286	£3106
	Carl MASON	Eng	72	73	69	72	286	£3106
29	Keith WATERS	Eng	66	75	72	74	287	£2437
	Peter MITCHELL	Eng	76	70	72	69	287	£2437
	Jim RUTLEDGE	Can	71	73	71	72	287	£2437
	Antonio GARRIDO	Sp	74	69	71	73	287	£2437
	Marc Antoine FARRY	Fr	72	70	73	72	287	£2437
	Eamonn DARCY	Ire	73	73	73	68	287	£2437
35	Bill MALLEY	USA	75	71	69	73	288	£2097
	Santiago LUNA	Sp	72	74	71	71	288	£2097
	Gordon J BRAND	Eng	74	71	73	70	288	£2097
	Brian MARCHBANK	Scot	69	75	73	71	288	£2097
	Mark MOULAND	Wal	67	74	75	72	288	£2097
40	Christy O' CONNOR Jr	Ire	71	74	72	72	289	£1785
	Mats HALLBERG	Swe	72	71	71	75	289	£1785
	Jose-Maria CANIZARES	Sp	72	69	76	72	289	£1785
	Mitch ADCOCK	USA	76	70	68	75	289	£1785
	Tony CHARNLEY	Eng	73	73	75	68	289	£1785
	Brian WATTS	USA	71	73	73	72	289	£1785
46	Mike CLAYTON	Aus	74	69	76	71	290	£1473
	Glenn RALPH	Eng	74	70	72	74	290	£1473
	John BLAND	SA	73	71	77	69	290	£1473
	Martin POXON	Eng	73	70	70	77	290	£1473
	Jimmy HEGGARTY	N.Ire	75	71	72	72	290	£1473
51	Mike SMITH	USA	74	69	74	74	291	£1105
	Gordon BRAND Jr	Scot	71	75	71	74	291	£1105
	David A RUSSELL	Eng	76	68	72	75	291	£1105
	Marc PENDARIES	Fr	73	71	75	72	291	£1105
	Mark JAMES	Eng	70	76	75	70	291	£1105
	Hugh BAIOCCHI	SA	73	71	75	72	291	£1105
	Barry LANE	Eng	73	72	73	73	291	£1105
	Patrice LEGLISE	Fr	71	75	73	72	291	£1105
59	Michael KING	Eng	74	71	75	72	292	£836
	Neil HANSEN	Eng	74	71	74	73	292	£836
	Peter FOWLER	Aus	69	76	74	73	292	£836
	Wayne SMITH	Aus	74	72	73	73	292	£836
63	Philip PARKIN	Wal	73	73	75	72	293	£751
	Steen TINNING	Den	73	68	74	78	293	£751
65	Jamie HOWELL	USA	73	70	81	70	294	£708
66	Jeff HALL	Eng	74	72	77	72	295	£283
67	Jean VAN DE VELDE	Fr	71	74	75	77	297	£281
68	Gery WATINE	Fr	71	75	76	76	298	£279
69	Emanuele BOLOGNESI	It	76	70	76	77	299	£277
70	Ross MCFARLANE	Eng	72	73	77	79	301	£275

RIVERO'S
gamble beats the odds

JOSE RIVERO TOOK A CHANCE ON A NEW PUTTER IN MONTE CARLO AND REAPED A HANDSOME REWARD AS A RESULT.

One ounce and three degrees made all the difference to Jose Rivero in the Monte Carlo Open.

If there was any doubt that modern tournament golf is a game of such fractions it was removed when the Spaniard arrived in Monaco and conducted an inquest on his failure to make a presentable defence of his French Open title. Rivero had departed after two rounds for the second week running and was puzzled as to why he had putted so poorly. It did not take fellow Madrileno, Manuel Pinero, very long to find the answer. He examined Rivero's putter, which had been fitted with a graphite shaft earlier in the season. Pinero diagnosed the putter was too light and advised his friend to discard it and look for a club closer in characteristics to the one he had first used when he ventured on to the Tour in 1983.

By sheer good fortune such a putter resided in the Mont Agel professional's shop and was available for a consideration of 500 francs. Its steel shaft provided the extra weight and a visit to the vice in the Tour workshop gave it the additional loft Rivero required to be confident on the ball. Just how many happy returns he was to enjoy for his £50 investment was to become clear as the tournament unfolded.

Nick Faldo, savouring his return to the top of the European money list by virtue of his Chantilly smash-and-grab was talking about that 'winning feeling' Seve Ballesteros, Tom Watson and Jack Nicklaus know all about. It was something he wished to cultivate. The Englishman was making his first visit to the millionaires' playground but there was still no place like home. He was happy to pay his taxes and would

not dream of trying to become a fiscal exile. He might have been thinking of Ballesteros who was at 'home' having recently become a Monte Carlo resident and a privileged member of Monaco's array of jet-set sporting ambassadors. The Spaniard played as usual with Prince Rainier in the pro-am and there were other important social commitments for him to fulfil.

Mark McNulty, Rodger Davis and defending champion Peter Senior helped to constitute a formidable invasion force, but Ballesteros confirmed local expectations by going straight to the front with a 65. He was joined by the Swede Jesper Parnevik, England's Andrew Sherborne and, less surprisingly, a revitalised Rivero.

Sherborne would have been out on his own but for falling victim to Rule 16–2. His 12-foot putt for a birdie three at the sixth stopped on the rim of the hole, overhanging the cup. As Sherborne approached to knock in his ball, it dropped of its own accord. His delight with the delayed birdie was soon dispelled when both his partners, French-

man Frederic Regard and England's Mike McLean, declared that the ball had been at rest longer than the 10 seconds permitted under Rule 16. Sherborne had to add a penalty stroke to the three shots he had actually taken and accept a par four on his card. He took the decision with good grace, agreeing that his partners were better judges of the time that had elapsed.

Time, or to be strictly accurate, circadian disrhythmia, caught up with Australian Ian Baker-Finch in the opening round. He had flown in overnight from Japan and went straight to the course to shoot 29 for the first nine holes. He took seven at the 10th and 42 strokes in all to get home, saying: 'It was a nice feeling while it lasted but then I woke up'.

Ability to leapfrog time zones is essential to the modern professional and so is patience. It can take a special type of the latter quality to stay serene on spectacular Mont Agl in June, particularly when the clouds sit stubbornly on the mountain top, visibility is cut to a few yards and golf becomes impossible. Frustration increases because 2500 feet below, the beaches remain bathed in sunshine. Rivero was enveloped by one such cloud after playing 17 holes of his second round in 60 strokes. He had to wait three hours before the fog lifted to allow him to add a par four for a halfway total of 129.

Earlier the sun had shone continuously on McNulty whose 62, one shot outside the course record, gave him a 10 under par 128 and put him eight strokes ahead of Faldo, despite a cultured 65 from the Open champion. Ballesteros played most of his round in heavy rain and 66 left him three behind the Zimbabwean.

The fickle weather was all too much for Chris Moody. He became so disenchanted with his lack of success on the greens that he consigned his putter to a watery grave, hurling the offending club into the pond guarding the approach to the 18th — and refused to sign his card.

It might have been more profitable to follow the example of Lyndsay Stephen, a genial Australian who was experiencing similar problems. His tee shot to the 154 yards 14th pitched straight into the hole — then spun straight out. Stephen chose to regard the incident as an omen of impending good fortune. His luck duly turned that evening during a visit to the world-famous casino with fellow Australian Bob Shearer. They won £500 for a £5 stake by coming up with a Royal Flush at the poker tables. Stephen shot 62 the next day, went on to finish fourth and took home more than £10,000. Who said gambling was a vice?

By the end of the third round McNulty and Rivero on 196 had drawn two clear of Ballesteros with Faldo and Senior both nine behind. The title lay between the leading trio. Ballesteros looked to hold all the psychological advantages when he birdied the 14th to draw level with Rivero at 13 under par, with McNulty one behind. Ahead lay a short par four of 285 yards that he had birdied in each previous round, by relying on his peerless short game. On this occasion Ballesteros put his faith in his driver. It was as though the spirit of his daredevil youth had suddenly resumed control. In going boldly for an eagle he could deliver the knock-out blow there and then. Instead, it was the matador who was the victim as he hooked his drive into bushes. Ballesteros took six and lost three strokes to both his rivals.

Rivero's new putter then once again proved its worth with its 22nd birdie of the week at the 17th and his 65 gave him victory by two strokes from McNulty. Ballesteros was another three behind but his stock was rising. His relationship with his new English caddie Ian Wright was on a sound footing and his putting had improved markedly.

Rivero sported a smile as wide as the first fairway. Investments that yield a return of 700–1 are not exactly commonplace. He was a long way from breaking the Bank of Monte Carlo — but a £35,000 jackpot would do very nicely.

Rivero recovers

Sun, sea and greens

Monte Carlo pageantry as the winner meets Prince Ranier

POS	NAME	CTRY	1	2	3	4	TOTAL	PRIZE MONEY
1	Jose RIVERO	Sp	65	64	67	65	261	£35013
2	Mark MCNULTY	Zim	66	62	68	67	263	£23342
3	Severiano BALLESTEROS	Sp	65	66	67	68	266	£13151
4	Lyndsay STEPHEN	Aus	72	68	62	66	268	£10504
5	Hugh BAIOCCHI	SA	67	68	67	68	270	£8887
6	Nick FALDO	Eng	71	65	69	67	272	£7352
7	Bob E SMITH	USA	71	67	68	67	273	£5777
	Jeff HAWKES	SA	66	70	71	66	273	£5777
9	Gavin LEVENSON	SA	67	66	70	71	274	£4445
	Peter SENIOR	Aus	70	68	67	69	274	£4445
11	Craig PARRY	Aus	68	65	68	74	275	£3209
	Manuel CALERO	Sp	69	67	71	68	275	£3209
	Michael ALLEN	USA	69	71	70	65	275	£3209
	Bob SHEARER	Aus	73	67	65	70	275	£3209
	Andrew SHERBORNE	Eng	65	69	72	69	275	£3209
	Peter TERAVAINEN	USA	72	64	68	71	275	£3209
	Magnus PERSSON	Swe	68	69	65	73	275	£3209
	Antonio GARRIDO	Sp	68	68	68	71	275	£3209
19	Jerry HAAS	USA	67	69	69	71	276	£2429
	Colin MONTGOMERIE	Scot	69	68	72	67	276	£2429
	Costantino ROCCA	it	73	67	68	68	276	£2429
	Richard BOXALL	Eng	68	69	70	69	276	£2429
	Emilio RODRIGUEZ	Sp	69	64	73	70	276	£2429
	Wayne STEPHENS	Eng	74	66	70	66	276	£2429
25	Mitch ADCOCK	USA	66	75	67	69	277	£2016
	Frederic REGARD	Fr	70	66	67	74	277	£2016
	Philip PARKIN	Wal	73	67	69	68	277	£2016
	Ian BAKER-FINCH	Aus	71	68	68	70	277	£2016
	Jim RUTLEDGE	Can	70	66	69	72	277	£2016
	Manuel PINERO	Sp	74	64	70	69	277	£2016
	Mark MOULAND	Wal	68	68	67	74	277	£2016
32	Miguel MARTIN	Sp	72	67	70	69	278	£1701
	Glenn RALPH	Eng	69	69	72	68	278	£1701
	Anders SORENSEN	Den	67	69	70	72	278	£1701
	Paul KENT	Eng	72	69	67	70	278	£1701
	Silvio GRAPPASONNI	It	69	69	66	75	279	£1554
	Grant TURNER	Eng	72	68	68	71	279	£1554
	Jerry ANDERSON	Can	71	70	69	69	279	£1554
39	Ian ROBERTS	Aus	71	69	69	71	280	£1386
	Mike HARWOOD	Aus	72	67	70	71	280	£1386
	David WILLIAMS	Eng	67	70	72	71	280	£1386
	Joe HIGGINS	Eng	66	71	71	72	280	£1386
	Philip WALTON	Ire	70	71	69	70	280	£1386
44	John SLAUGHTER	USA	74	67	70	70	281	£1239
	Glyn DAVIES	Wal	67	73	67	74	281	£1239
46	Ron COMMANS	USA	70	71	69	72	282	£1113
	Derrick COOPER	Eng	71	69	70	72	282	£1113
	Paul CURRY	Eng	67	68	74	73	282	£1113
	Gery WATINE	Fr	68	70	74	70	282	£1113
50	Bryan NORTON	USA	71	69	71	72	283	£945
	Wraith GRANT	Eng	74	67	71	71	283	£945
	Craig MCCLELLAN	USA	70	67	72	74	283	£945
	Benoit DUCOULOMBIER	Fr	69	68	72	74	283	£945
54	Wayne SMITH	Aus	72	68	73	71	284	£777
	Bill MALLEY	USA	68	73	72	71	284	£777
	Jean VAN DE VELDE	Fr	69	68	71	76	284	£777
	Tim PLANCHIN	Fr	69	70	68	77	284	£777
58	Peter FOWLER	Aus	69	72	69	75	285	£640
	Craig LAURENCE	Eng	70	70	73	72	285	£640
	Bryan LEWIS	Scot	68	67	75	75	285	£640
	Ross MCFARLANE	Eng	74	67	70	74	285	£640
62	Lee JONES	Eng	70	70	75	71	286	£588
63	Jesper PARNEVIK	Swe	65	74	75	73	287	£567
64	Ronald STELTEN	USA	69	70	73	76	288	£546
65	Frederic MARTIN	Fr	70	70	71	78	289	£525
66	John BLAND	SA	71	69	73	77	290	£210
67	Stephen MCALLISTER	Scot	69	70	80	72	291	£207
	Per-Arne BROSTEDT	Swe	73	66	75	77	291	£207
69	Andrew COTTON	Eng	70	71	75	77	293	£204
70	Jean-Bernard LECUONA	Fr	71	70	81	73	295	£201
	Andrew CHANDLER	Eng	75	66	78	76	295	£201
72	John O'LEARY	Ire	72	69	RETD			£198

Room to manouvre for
Roger Chapman

American imports Mark O'Meara and Ben Crenshaw bit off more than they could chew

Tony Johnstone and son on the nursery slopes

POS	NAME	CTRY	1	2	3	4	TOTAL	PRIZE MONEY
1	Barry LANE	Eng	70	67	66	68	271	£41660
2	Sandy LYLE	Scot	68	69	69	68	274	£21705
	Jose RIVERO	Sp	64	70	72	68	274	£21705
4	Roger CHAPMAN	Eng	68	68	67	72	275	£12500
5	Peter FOWLER	Aus	71	63	69	73	276	£10600
6	Mats LANNER	Swe	71	71	72	63	277	£8125
	Jose-Maria OLAZABAL	Sp	71	70	67	69	277	£8125
8	David GRAHAM	Aus	71	69	70	68	278	£5362
	Rodger DAVIS	Aus	74	66	68	70	278	£5362
	David GILFORD	Eng	69	70	70	69	278	£5362
	Russell WEIR	Scot	66	72	67	73	278	£5362
12	Mark O'MEARA	USA	70	69	67	73	279	£4046
	Mike HARWOOD	Aus	68	65	75	71	279	£4046
	Ian WOOSNAM	Wal	68	71	71	69	279	£4046
15	Stephen BENNETT	Eng	69	65	76	70	280	£3521
	Fred COUPLES	USA	64	68	72	76	280	£3521
	Denis DURNIAN	Eng	70	67	71	72	280	£3521
18	Mark JAMES	Eng	74	69	69	69	281	£3062
	Wayne SMITH	Aus	67	72	67	75	281	£3062
	Howard CLARK	Eng	70	69	73	69	281	£3062
	Anders FORSBRAND	Swe	71	71	68	71	281	£3062
22	Ian BAKER-FINCH	Aus	70	67	75	70	282	£2700
	Hugh BAIOCCHI	SA	69	72	71	70	282	£2700
	Payne STEWART	USA	68	70	71	73	282	£2700
	Noel RATCLIFFE	Aus	68	71	69	74	282	£2700
	Bill MCCOLL	Scot	72	70	70	70	282	£2700
27	Peter SENIOR	Aus	69	72	71	71	283	£2437
	Craig PARRY	Aus	70	68	73	72	283	£2437
29	David FEHERTY	N.Ire	69	72	70	73	284	£2150
	Tommy ARMOUR III	USA	72	69	71	72	284	£2150
	Colin MONTGOMERIE	Scot	69	72	72	71	284	£2150
	Carl MASON	Eng	73	68	69	74	284	£2150
	Gordon BRAND Jr	Scot	71	72	69	72	284	£2150
	Brian MARCHBANK	Scot	74	68	73	69	284	£2150
35	Peter MITCHELL	Eng	72	71	71	71	285	£1875
	John DE FOREST	USA	72	69	75	69	285	£1875
	Mike CLAYTON	Aus	72	69	75	69	285	£1875
	Frank NOBILO	NZ	69	73	74	69	285	£1875
39	Emmanuel DUSSART	Fr	74	68	70	74	286	£1625
	Vaughan SOMERS	Aus	71	70	72	73	286	£1625
	Mats HALLBERG	Swe	65	76	70	75	286	£1625
	Michael ALLEN	USA	70	71	71	74	286	£1625
	Robert LEE	Eng	69	71	71	75	286	£1625
	Sam TORRANCE	Scot	68	72	73	73	286	£1625
45	Jose-Maria CANIZARES	Sp	70	71	74	72	287	£1325
	Tony CHARNLEY	Eng	68	69	75	75	287	£1325
	Andrew SHERBORNE	Eng	71	67	73	76	287	£1325
	Philip PARKIN	Wal	71	69	74	73	287	£1325
	Peter TERAVAINEN	USA	70	72	70	75	287	£1325
	Des SMYTH	Ire	70	72	74	71	287	£1325
51	Ken BROWN	Scot	69	72	72	75	288	£1075
	Neil COLES	Eng	73	70	71	74	288	£1075
	Eamonn DARCY	Ire	71	70	72	75	288	£1075
	Gordon J BRAND	Eng	69	69	73	77	288	£1075
55	David J RUSSELL	Eng	70	73	73	73	289	£900
	Fulton ALLEM	SA	70	71	72	76	289	£900
	Mark MOULAND	Wal	70	68	74	77	289	£900
58	Philip HARRISON	Eng	68	74	75	73	290	£762
	Derrick COOPER	Eng	70	72	75	73	290	£762
	Neal BRIGGS	Eng	72	71	72	75	290	£762
	Tom KITE Jr	USA	72	71	74	73	290	£762
62	Malcolm MACKENZIE	Eng	67	73	75	76	291	£687
	Michael KING	Eng	69	73	70	79	291	£687
64	Magnus SUNESSON	Swe	69	74	72	77	292	£650
65	Ross DRUMMOND	Scot	75	68	74	77	294	£625
66	Jamie HOWELL	USA	73	70	74	83	300	£249
	Robert RICHARDSON	SA	71	70	81	78	300	£249

Brollies and brooding hills frame the action

THE MAN
in blue

*i*n the final round of the 1986 US Masters Severiano Ballesteros stood in the middle of the 15th fairway nursing a comfortable two shot lead. In spite of his position in the tournament there was not much ebullience in his play. He had been deeply affected by the death of his father, Baldomero, earlier in the year and believed that this family tragedy was a portent of worse to come in his chosen profession.

Standing in the middle of that Augusta fairway, Ballesteros had plenty of time to ponder. Ahead of him on the green was Bernhard Langer, who had never been noted for his speed, while one hole ahead of Langer was Jack Nicklaus who had previously eagled the 15th and had just put his tee shot to the short 16th within a few feet of the hole. The cheers and yells from a partisan crowd echoed through the Georgia pines as Nicklaus performed these heroics and they did nothing to help Ballesteros. After what seemed like an age, the green was finally clear and he could play. He selected a four iron, plenty of club for the job, and decided to hit a high, soft shot which would land gently on the shallow green, thereby setting up the birdie on this par five hole of 520 yards and putting him in an unassailable position.

The shot was horrible. With an uncharacteristic lurch Ballesteros sent his ball into the lake which fronts the 15th green and drowned his hopes for the title. His spirits plunged too – fate had decreed that 1986 was going to be a bad year and here was the confirmation.

The inner battle was to continue for two more years. Even though during that period he had enough successes to

AFTER FOUR YEARS WITHOUT A MAJOR CHAMPION-SHIP WIN, THERE WAS AN AIR OF DESPERATION ABOUT SEVE BALLESTEROS. BUT WITH ONE OF THE GREATEST FINAL ROUNDS IN THE HISTORY OF THE OPEN, DESPAIR TURNED INTO DELIGHT AS HE WAS REUNITED WITH THE OLD CLARET JUG FOR THE THIRD TIME IN HIS CAREER.

satisfy most professionals for a lifetime, further major titles eluded him and the more they eluded him, the deeper became the brooding and the more his confidence was sapped.

Matters had not improved much at the start of the 1988 season. Beset by putting problems, Ballesteros hardly featured in the US Masters and had faded in the US Open at Brookline. There had been signs of rehabilitation, chiefly at the 1987 Ryder Cup when he had really got his teeth into his favourite pastime – eating Americans for breakfast – but a more significant step was taken when Ballesteros took on 40-year old Ian Wright from Redcar as caddie.

All of Ballesteros' four previous major championship wins had been in the company of English-speaking professional caddies. Since his last victory at St Andrews in the 1984 Open Championship, he had employed one of his brothers to caddie in the majors. The emotional involvement was too high. Arguments broke out at frequent intervals during a round; animated exchanges would develop containing a great deal of gesticulating and the effect was invariably destructive. Wright's dispassionate, down-to-earth attitude was in complete contrast to the Ballesteros temperament and, furthermore, Wright only took the job on his terms from a man who is notoriously hard on his caddies. From the outset Wright insisted that Ballesteros should try and relax more and enjoy his golf and that a smile or two on the golf course would not go amiss either.

Thus it was that Ballesteros arrived at Royal Lytham & St Annes for the 117th Open Golf Championship to prepare for what was certainly his best opportunity to break his victory drought in the Grand Slam events. Nine years previously he had sent European golf into its current stratospheric orbit when he had, at the age of 22, become the youngest winner of the Open since Tom Morris back in the days of the cleek and the rut-iron. Returning to the site of that momentous victory would surely provide extra incentive to the man who was recognised as the outstanding talent of his generation.

Lytham is a rarity among the links courses used for the Open in that the sea cannot be glimpsed from any of its holes and it is surrounded by the red-brick edifices of well-to-do suburbia. Its quality as a Championship test is

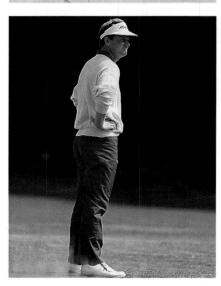

feat was very nearly emulated by David J. Russell whose opening shot hit the pin, leaving the ball on the edge of the hole. Russell was playing with Jack Nicklaus and this prospect had made him a nervous wreck prior to starting. Russell's wife had asked if there was anything she could do. 'Yes,' replied her husband, 'take me home.' Russell's golf, however, belied his emotions and he reached the turn in a mere 29 strokes. 'Now come back in 29', said Nicklaus on the 10th tee but an unlucky bounce over a boundary fence at the 12th put paid to that and Russell staggered home in 40 for a 69.

With three former Open champions breathing down his neck, the pressure was all on Price. Ballesteros stated after the third round that the winner would be the man who could take the pressure best while Lyle pointed out that par golf was not going to win, a round of 68 or 69 was needed.

In almost every case Lyle's prediction would have been correct but he had failed to take into account the genius of Ballesteros. Seve emerged for the final round dressed in the same dark blue ensemble that he had worn when he won in 1979 but the sense of *deja vu* did not really emerge until the seventh. At this stage Ballesteros and Faldo were six under par, Price seven under. First Ballesteros eagled then Price followed him in from slightly nearer. Poor Faldo, after a fine second shot, was blocked out from the flag by a large mound and the three putts which followed put his further efforts on an increasingly token basis.

The putt at the seventh seemed to inspire Ballesteros, for he birdied the eighth, the 10th and 11th to draw ahead of Price. A dropped shot at the 12th put them level again and then Price nearly holed his second to the 13th. Ballesteros holed from 18 feet for a matching three and so the two provided a marvellous exhibition of thrust and counter-thrust over the closing holes. The most telling blow came from Ballesteros at, appropriately, the 16th. On this hole in 1979 in the midst of his madcap dance to victory, he had hit his drive among some parked cars and then pocketed an outrageous birdie three with a pitch and a long putt. On this occasion the approach was totally orthodox – a one iron to the middle of the fairway followed by a nine iron which left the ball a matter of inches from the hole. Price could not match this birdie but he did not buckle, hitting a wonderful one iron to the heart of the 17th green to keep Ballesteros in sight.

Where did the hole go? Paul Azinger reflects on a missed opportunity

Sir: Has anyone noticed the resemblance between Roger Chapman and Tom Kite? Are they by any chance related? I think we should be told

Caddie Ian Wright confirms yardage to a quizzical employer

Local exhortation at Lytham

A chip off a block of spectators from Nick Price

BALLESTEROS
lands another title

FOLLOWING HIS OPEN CHAMPION-SHIP VICTORY SEVERIANO BALLESTEROS RELAXED BY GOING FISHING THEN MARKED HIS RETURN BY CATCHING ANOTHER BIG PRIZE IN SWEDEN.

Seve Ballesteros put the 'Gone Fishing' sign above his door after his victory in the Open Championship. He had returned to Pedrena to a hero's welcome. 'The people of the village had been waiting four years to let off their fireworks again and they were not going to wait any longer' he remarked.

When the celebrations subsided the Spaniard turned to his favourite relaxation and took out a boat into the shallows of the estuary below the golf course. The solitude helped him to recharge the batteries. Every bite was as satisfying as a good tee shot but as a fisherman Seve agreed he was a high handicapper. He would go hungry if he had to depend on his prowess as an angler.

The few days messing about on the river, and the occasional cycle ride to tone up his leg muscles, had left him refreshed and ready for the next challenge. He was returning to Sweden and the Scandinavian Enterprise Open for the first time in five years. There had, however, been a price to pay. In order to satisfy the apartheid-conscious Swedish authorities Ballesteros had been required to give certain assurances. He had put his name to a letter which indicated to Swedish sports officials that he had no intention of returning to play golf in South Africa. All South Africans had been excluded from the tournament in Stockholm but a blanket embargo on all golfers who had ever competed in the Republic had been delayed for a further 12 months.

With the formalities completed the Open champion was ready for a return to work and the enthusiastic Swedish golf fans flocked out to scenic Drottning-holm to see the maestro.

Ballesteros did not disappoint. From the outset he looked eager to net another title and scored eight birdies in the first 12 holes of his opening round. He started at the 10th and covered the opening half in just 31 strokes. Then he sank a chip at the first and birdied the next two holes as well from putts of around 20 feet.

Golf was being made to look the simplest of games by a master of its arts. However, even Steve Davies mis-cues occasionally and Ballesteros proved he was mortal at the drive-and-pitch fourth, his 13th. He left himself an approach of 120 metres to the flag and selected a nine-iron for the standard shot. His ball landed in deep rough 25 metres behind the green — the signal for caddie Ian Wright to be subjected to a searching Spanish inquisition. After pointedly pacing out the distance from his divot to the target, Seve agreed that Mr Wright had been exactly right with his assessment. He had simply hit the ball too hard and too well. What was

incontestable was that the spell was broken. The Open champion dropped three strokes to the card in the last six holes to return 67 instead of the 62 he had deemed possible. 'I had the course by the throat' he commented 'but then it took hold of my throat.'

Craig Parry's record-matching 64, containing an inward 30, subsequently led the field from England's Mark Davis and the Ryder Cup pair, Eamonn Darcy and Gordon Brand Junior on 65. Former US Masters champion Craig Stadler and David J. Russell had 68, the Englishman having been reunited at the last minute with his golf clubs. Russell had just experienced the modern travellers' nightmare — an airline computer which refused to recognise his existence or, although he possessed a baggage ticket, his golf bag. He feared for the welfare of his tools of the trade but they were located in Turin and restored to their owner 24 hours after his arrival, none the worse for their diversion.

Parry's 64 was equalled by Yorkshire's Simon Townend in round two, and in the process the 24-year old from Leeds took a share of a world record. Townend had only eight putts in his outward half, twice chipping in, then single-putting five of the other seven holes. Only two other professionals, Americans Jim Colbert and Sam Trahan, have ever been as economical on the greens. Not-so-simple Simon totalled only 20 putts in his entire career-best performance, two more than the lowest officially recognized.

It was still not enough to prevent Graham Marsh, still an effective campaigner at 44, from taking the halfway lead. Marsh also found form with his putter, holing three 10-yarders in a second 66 to head Parry and two more

Australians Peter Senior and Gerry Taylor.

The third round of a tournament is, by necessity, an opportunity to take stock. For the majority the avoidance of the halfway cut is in itself an achievement. Consolidation becomes the priority as the pack husbands its resources for 'pay day', the final round which determines the size of the week's cheque.

Ballesteros is among those who scorn such caution. For him it is the time to attack, to aim for the unassailable lead. A deft chip to eight feet gave him a birdie at the first and another came at the seventh before a stunning four iron shot from around 200 yards ended four feet from the eighth flag for an eagle three and an outward 32. He was round in 66 for a 13 under par 203 that left him one shot off a lead which resided with the man whose clubs had been to Italy — the aforementioned Russell.

'D.J.' holds the distinction of being the youngest golfer to hole in one in the Open Championship, having struck the perfect shot at the Postage Stamp, Troon in 1973 when he was 19.

Ace number 11 of the Russell career arrived at Drottningholm's sixth hole, courtesy of his seven iron — and it put him firmly into heavy metal! The special award for the feat was a lorry load of steel — 15 tons to be exact — valued at £9,000.

Russell chose the cash alternative and began to wonder if his luck would hold. His 66 for 202 gave him the honour of leading the field into the last circuit, in which he would partner Ballesteros. Gordon Brand Junior was in third place, a shot behind the Spaniard on 204. That was as close as anyone came to thwarting a majestic Seve who swept into a five stroke lead by the final turn. Russell's slide to a 77 and eventual 10th place began when he missed a two foot putt at the 5th and took two shots in greenside sand at the sixth. He went out in 40 to 34 by Ballesteros.

Four homeward birdies sent the Open champion speeding to a closing 67 and the 53rd victory of his career by a conclusive five shot margin. He had turned his first public appearance since Lytham into a lap of honour. There was only one drawback — the clubs he had wielded with such distinction over the last four years were now worn out.

Ballesteros announced that he intended to present them for auction, with charity the benefactor. 'They are extra long and extra strong' he said. 'Whoever buys them will need to be a tall, strong man if he wants to use them. But one thing is sure — his handicap will come down very quickly!'

Gordon Brand Junior stooped but didn't conquer

Home hope Magnus Persson

Dreaming of the future?

Craig Stadler falls foul
of the walrus trap

BAKER

soars with the eagles

*P*eter Baker went from one mishap to another on his first professional venture in the August of 1986. The airline he travelled with to the PLM Open in Sweden lost his clubs and then when they turned up he broke his driver. Then he missed the 36 hole cut by a shot. Two years to the week later, Baker could afford to smile at such setbacks. At Fulford, York, he won his first professional tournament, the Benson and Hedges International Open, with a style and swagger he will find difficult to match if he follows it up with another 50 such victories.

Baker was 20 when he won – he has now celebrated his 21st birthday – and for many of those years he has carried one of those labels people always stick to young golfers of promise. In Baker's case it was 'the next Sandy Lyle.'

At 5 feet 9 inches tall and 11 stone he bears as much resemblance to Lyle as Laurel did to Hardy. Yet the comparison carries some validity. Baker is coached by Sandy's father, Alex, and their careers have followed parallel lines. As amateurs, both won the English Stroke-Play Championship. Both played Walker Cup golf. Both were rookie professionals of the year and both won their first tournaments the following season. The most extraordinary fact is that Baker achieved all these things exactly one year earlier than Sandy Lyle.

They are also two-thirds of a remarkable contribution that Shropshire has made to modern golf. Both were born in and played amateur golf for England's smallest county, Lyle doing so alongside Ian Woosnam. Now, having already provided two of the best players of the current decade, Shropshire, in Baker,

WHEN TONY JACKLIN COINED THE PHRASE 'ONE OF THE BOYS' IN 1987 TO DESCRIBE SOME OF THE YOUNGER PLAYERS ON TOUR HE ALSO CLAIMED THEY WERE CONTENT TO WIN MONEY NOT TROPHIES. JACKLIN EXEMPTED PETER BAKER FROM SUCH CRITICISM, SAYING HE WOULD WIN A TOURNAMENT WITHIN TWO YEARS. HE WAS RIGHT.

may have unearthed the player of the nineties.

Such talk became commonplace following his success at York. To win at 20 was a rare enough achievement. But it was the manner of victory that led to Nick Faldo describing Baker as 'exactly the sort of player the Tour needs. He is easily the best of the next generation of British professionals.' All through a fascinating last day, the tall Londoner was in front and another win was within touching distance standing on the 15th tee. For 32 holes he had been paired with Baker. They had played the first 18 of those in 66 strokes each but now experience appeared to be telling. Faldo had a three stroke lead.

It was not how Baker saw it. He was still thinking of victory. 'I need three birdies to make a play-off,' he told his caddie, Peter Newbury. He made the equivalent of three birdies but that does not do justice to the spectacular way he picked up those strokes to par. First the 15th, where Faldo missed from 4 feet for par and Baker holed from 3 feet for a birdie. Now the deficit was just one, which was how it remained as they came to the last hole. Ahead, two more young players, the 22-year old Spaniard Jose-Maria Olazabal and the Australian Craig Parry, had set a 16 under par total of 272. Olazabal had finished with rounds of 66 and 65 and Parry had eagled the last. It meant that to beat them Faldo needed a birdie, and Baker an eagle.

Fulford is loved by all the professionals. It panders to their egos. It has generous target areas and its immaculate condition flatters their play and adds up to scores in the 60s. No hole is more generous than the last, a par five of just 488 yards in length. So the target set was perfectly realistic, even if it was a bit much asking a 20-year old, under the circumstances, to achieve an eagle.

Baker did it. Faldo got his birdie. For the first time since the first tee, the pair were level once more. Baker went into the play-off knowing he had nothing to lose. 'Everyone was looking for Nick's experience to tell,' he said. It did not. Baker played with a lack of inhibition attributable to youth. At the second extra hole, again the 18th, he hit a drive 290 yards, a five iron 20 feet from the pin and quite miraculously holed once more for an eagle for victory. And all this happened under the noses of his sponsors, who had a hospitality tent

No prizes for runner-up Nick Faldo as he chips to the 14th

Board games at the start of the final round

around the 18th green. How they charged their glasses all week! Baker played the hole: eagle, birdie, birdie, eagle, eagle.

Baker's first full season saw him named Rookie of the Year, but he was far from content. He had started the year finishing third in the opening event, the Moroccan Open, and straight away had made enough money to keep his player's card. But after that there were no such high finishes. Gradually he turned to the bosom of his older circle of friends. He sought the counsel of people like David J Russell and Ian Woosnam. 'I cannot explain it but I started to feel better on the first tee,' he said. Baker once more started the season well. He got into contention in the Portuguese Open. 'It was a nice feeling,' he said. 'It was one I wanted to taste more and more.'

It was shortly after the Open Championship that he started to play really well, averaging six birdies a round. He was piecing everything together and by the time he came to Fulford he was ready and he knew it. 'Sure I can win,' he said after the second round.

As the sun dropped on a memorable Benson and Hedges International Open, everyone was sure he would win again. Record crowds basked in golden weather, great golf, and the introduction of a young man destined perhaps for greatness. No-one could ask for more.

Panoramic view of the 14th green

And coming into the ditch at the 17th it's Peter Baker in the lead . . .

. . . followed by Nick Faldo a few lengths behind . . .

. . . and just behind him Sandy Lyle making close order . . .

. . . with Malcolm Mackenzie well to the back of the field.

62 O CONNOR JR
65 TURNER
67 CHARNLEY
    CALERO
    O LEARY
    DURNIAN

O'Connor exults . . .

Faldo swings . . .

*Mark McNulty on
the 18th*

Marsh ponders . . .   *while James sweats it out . . .*

NOBILO'S
victory is gripping stuff

AN OVERDOSE OF CASTOR OIL ON HIS GRIPS RESULTED IN A REMARKABLE OPENING ROUND FROM FRANK NOBILO WHO THEN WENT ON TO BECOME THE SEVENTH NEW WINNER OF THE SEASON.

*t*he dictionary describes it as a colourless or yellow glutinous substance obtained from the seeds of a euphorbiaceous plant. A regular spoonful was once considered essential to keep the British nation on its toes and most senior citizens can recall its devastating efficiency when it was in vogue during their early schooldays.

It is almost the last thing one would choose as a catalyst for winning golf but New Zealand's Frank Nobilo demonstrated its remarkable properties when he became the seventh new champion of the season at Flommens in August.

It, for readers with short memories, is that favourite Victorian purgative, castor oil. Prudently, Frank did not take it himself — he gave it to his golf clubs. The reason why is best known to another antipodean, Lyndsay Stephen, the Australian who found a Royal Flush in the casino at Monte Carlo. Nobilo suffers from dermatitis and uses leather rather than rubber grips on his clubs. By the time he arrived in southern Sweden for the PLM Open those grips had become hard and shiny with constant use and were badly in need of refreshment.

Nobilo and Stephen had travelled together and the latter casually mentioned that he had read somewhere that Jack Nicklaus cleaned his leather grips with castor oil. So on the eve of the tournament Nobilo set out from his Malmo hotel to purchase a bottle of the cathartic. Three hours later he had managed to track down his quarry and then repaired to his bedroom to administer the treatment.

He soaked a rag in the liquid and applied it to the ailing grips. Within minutes the state of the cloth provided convincing proof that he was on the right track. The grips became noticeably softer and were gradually regaining their original hue. But a little knowledge is a dangerous thing — especially where castor oil is concerned. Nobilo, once a competent cricketer, remembered that batsmen used to clean their bats and then leave them to stand overnight in a tray of linseed oil. He therefore reasoned that his golf club grips would benefit from similar immersion. So he poured the castor oil into a convenient plant holder and inserted the golf clubs, grip first.

In the morning he dropped them all into his golf bag and sped to the course in good time for his 9am first round start. First the New Zealander needed to find a caddie because his regular aide Steve Walsh had recently decided to seek fame and fortune with another master. A local replacement was found but was almost put out of action by his new employer's first practice shot at Flommens, one of three courses within Falsterbo's huge bird sanctuary. Nobilo introduced a new species, the Flying Wedge, as an oil-impregnated pitching club flew out of his hands when he struck the ball. It needed only a cursory examination to ascertain that the grip had become a gungy sponge, oozing castor oil at the slightest pressure. The Kiwi's spirits sank — there were 13 similar grips in his golf bag.

Stephen had transmitted only part of the Nicklaus recipe. The grips should first be thoroughly cleaned with an astringent, such as methylated spirit. Only then should castor oil be used — but sparingly. A smear on each grip will suffice, just enough to make the leather tacky. How the Auckland golfer held his game together to shoot a course record 63 that first morning will remain a secret between him and his Maker. It enabled him to lead from start to finish and not even a vigorous title defence by Howard Clark could shift Nobilo from pole position.

Clark had begun the week gaining first-hand knowledge of the growing strength of Swedish golf. He had captained a six-man Volvo Tour side against a team of Swedish professionals who won 2–1. Clark and Barry Lane, the new Scottish Open champion, had been scuppered by Mats Lanner and Magnus Persson who had combined to a better ball 59.

Yet the local knowledge of the Swedes was of doubtful benefit at Flommens where water, in the form of streams, ponds and sea inlets, is the dominant element. It comes into play on no less than 17 holes and for most was unavoidable. American John Slaughter had seven penalty strokes in a first

Local lad Johan Rystrom

round 76 and England's D.J. Russell counted six in a 73.

Even the admirably accurate Clark encountered a surfeit of H_2O. His tee shot at the 12th finished in a place where the only way to play the next shot was to paddle in the icy Baltic. Clark took off his shoes and socks and went in up to his knees. Howard's way saved par and he sailed to an opening 68.

By the halfway stage Nobilo had consolidated his lead with a follow-up 68 for 131, having successfully "de-castorised" his clubs by liberal use of towels. A stroke behind was Tony Charnley, followed by Sweden's Anders Forsbrand and Scottish rookie professional Colin Montgomerie who had opened with 66 and 67. Clark was six shots off the lead after a 69 for 137.

The cut came at two over par and at the 19th time of asking was survived by

Kent golfer, Michael McLean (68–73). There was no happier player in Sweden that week as he reflected on the irony of having travelled thousands of miles in search of a cure for his swing problems, only to find the answers within a five minutes walk of his home at Sevenoaks. A visit to his first teacher, the Knole Park club professional, Peter Gill, had done the trick.

A fierce crosswind sorted out the field in the third round which ended with Nobilo three shots ahead of Clark whose 68 was the lowest of the day. But when the New Zealander began his final round with a hat-trick of birdies to extend his lead to five shots the issue looked settled. Clark thought otherwise. He birdied four of the next five holes, Nobilo dropped a stroke at the sixth, and they were level at 10 under par at the turn. A birdie four at the 15th

Fans flocked to Flommens

put the Kiwi back into the lead but he was not assured of victory until the Ryder Cup man three-putted the short 17th from long range.

It was Nobilo's first European success and from first to last the former New Zealand PGA champion had been full of surprises. He had another up his sleeve. He had recently investigated his family tree and discovered that his ancestors had been members of a band of Italian pirates who had pillaged and plundered their way around the Adriatic and Yugoslavia before settling in New Zealand at the end of the 19th century.

Now he had made a name for himself in Europe in quite legitimate fashion. As he pointed out, golfers from "down under" have an additional handicap. 'When you come from so far away you have to climb so many

ladders' he said. 'All of us in New Zealand have lived for a decade in the shadow of our most famous golfer, Bob Charles. The time was overdue for one of us to make the limelight.'

Victory had given him a warm glow and it was time to celebrate, but first he had to have a word with a certain Australian about grip remedies.

First success for Frank Nobilo

Frank Nobilo, left, held off the challenge of Howard Clark, above

POS	NAME	CTRY	1	2	3	4	TOTAL	PRIZE MONEY
1	Frank NOBILO	NZ	63	68	71	68	270	£33126
2	Howard CLARK	Eng	68	69	68	66	271	£22064
3	Peter FOWLER	Aus	65	69	72	70	276	£10267
	Anders FORSBRAND	Swe	67	66	72	71	276	£10267
	Colin MONTGOMERIE	Scot	66	67	74	69	276	£10267
6	Ove SELLBERG	Swe	69	68	72	69	278	£6957
7	Anders SORENSEN	Den	69	68	71	71	279	£5963
8	Craig PARRY	Aus	67	67	76	70	280	£4094
	Tony CHARNLEY	Eng	66	66	76	72	280	£4094
	Magnus PERSSON	Swe	68	71	72	69	280	£4094
	Stephen BENNETT	Eng	72	69	67	72	280	£4094
	Mark MOULAND	Wal	68	74	69	69	280	£4094
13	Steen TINNING	Den	72	68	74	67	281	£3200
14	Matts HALLBERG	Swe	67	67	73	75	282	£2802
	Gordon J BRAND	Eng	70	69	74	69	282	£2802
	Jerry ANDERSON	Can	65	73	76	68	282	£2802
	Andrew MURRAY	Eng	70	71	71	70	282	£2802
	Vaughan SOMERS	Aus	70	72	71	69	282	£2802
19	Philip HARRISON	Eng	69	70	75	69	283	£2299
	David GILFORD	Eng	67	75	68	73	283	£2299
	Richard BOXALL	Eng	69	70	76	68	283	£2299
	Denis DURNIAN	Eng	66	72	71	74	283	£2299
	Bill MALLEY	USA	68	74	73	68	283	£2299
	Ronan RAFFERTY	N.Ire	72	69	73	69	283	£2299
	Olle KARLSSON	Swe	71	69	78	65	283	(AM)
25	Wayne RILEY	Aus	68	68	75	73	284	£2027
	Mats LANNER	Swe	67	68	77	72	284	£2027
	Simon BISHOP	Eng	68	69	75	72	284	£2027
28	David A RUSSELL	Eng	66	71	76	72	285	£1789
	Peter DAHLBERG	Swe	69	70	75	71	285	£1789
	Brett OGLE	Aus	70	70	75	70	285	£1789
	Mikael KARLSSON	Swe	72	70	73	70	285	£1789
	Magnus SUNESSON	Swe	70	68	75	72	285	£1789
33	Paul CARRIGILL	Eng	67	70	76	73	286	£1610
	Johan RYSTROM	Swe	66	72	77	71	286	£1610
35	Jeremy ROBINSON	Eng	69	67	80	71	287	£1470
	Alberto BINAGHI	It	72	70	69	76	287	£1470
	Paul KENT	Eng	70	72	73	72	287	£1470
	Paul CURRY	Eng	71	69	78	69	287	£1470
	Martin POXON	Eng	70	70	77	70	287	£1470
40	Costantino ROCCA	It	67	72	78	71	288	£1113
	Barry LANE	Eng	71	68	75	74	288	£1113
	Simon TOWNEND	Eng	70	71	75	72	288	£1113
	Peter PERSONS	USA	64	76	78	70	288	£1113
	Ruud BOS	Hol	71	70	77	70	288	£1113
	Keith WATERS	Eng	71	71	76	70	288	£1113
	Clas HULTMAN	Swe	70	71	75	72	288	£1113
	Per-Arne BROSTEDT	Swe	69	73	72	74	288	£1113
	Ross DRUMMOND	Scot	69	70	78	71	288	£1113
	Magnus GRANKVIST	Swe	71	71	74	72	288	£1113
	Andrew SHERBOURNE	Eng	72	70	74	72	288	£1113
	Mark ROE	Eng	71	69	75	73	288	£1113
	John HAWKSWORTH	Eng	71	71	74	72	288	£1113
53	Chip DRURY	USA	69	73	77	70	289	£775
	Stephen MCALLISTER	Scot	69	69	79	72	289	£775
	Kyi Hla HAN	Bur	69	70	77	73	289	£775
	Mike CLAYTON	Aus	73	69	72	75	289	£775
57	Derrick COOPER	Eng	69	72	79	70	290	£631
	Peter TERAVAINEN	USA	72	70	77	71	290	£631
	Luis CARBONETTI	Arg	66	75	81	68	290	£631
	James SPENCE	Eng	70	70	80	70	290	£631
	Peter HEDBLOM	Swe	67	69	78	76	290	(AM)
61	David WOOD	Wal	70	71	76	74	291	£566
	Magnus JONSSON	Swe	70	70	76	75	291	£566
63	Carl STROEMBERG	Swe	73	68	76	75	292	£536
64	Santiago LUNA	Spa	71	71	75	76	293	£404
	Peter CARSBO	Swe	68	73	80	72	293	£404
	Marc PENDARIES	Fra	73	67	75	78	293	£404
67	Jan TILMANIS	Swe	72	69	78	76	295	£198
	Per NYMAN	Swe	74	68	78	75	295	(AM)
68	Mark LITTON	Wal	71	69	82	75	297	£196
69	Michael MCLEAN	Eng	68	73	82	76	299	£194
70	Daniel WESTERMARK	Swe	69	72	81	80	302	£192

MOVING
ever closer to perfection

THE PERFECT ROUND OF GOLF IS BUT A DREAM. YET SEVERIANO BALLESTEROS ALMOST ACHIEVED THAT DREAM AS HE CAPTURED THE GERMAN OPEN AND CONTINUED HIS DOMINANCE OF THE TOUR.

*t*hat round was very close to being perfect,' said Severiano Ballesteros. 'No-one can play a perfect round but today I came close. Everything was on my side.' Ballesteros was purring over the last round of 62 with which he had cruised effortlessly to victory in the German Open.

There have been more memorable moments, more remarkable rounds. Who will ever forget St Andrews in 1984 when Ballesteros celebrated Open Championship victory by punching the air with joy? Or the way he accelerated audaciously to the Masters title in 1983? Ballesteros smacks his lips in self-appreciation when he recalls such treasured experiences. The Masters was magical, interwoven as it was with his worship of Augusta. And then St Andrews took this extraordinary Spaniard to a new high. 'To win at the home of golf on the last green was special, very special. I have never felt so emotional.'

But from that moment Ballesteros went through hell. He drowned in the water at Augusta in 1986 and one year later he was in tears there when he three-putted the first extra green. He went to court in Los Angeles, locked in a legal dispute with his first manager, and one major championship after another slipped past without his name being engraved on the silverware.

The Ballesteros who arrived at the Frankfurter course, only a couple of miles or so from the city centre, was a changed man. He had shed the monkey from his back and the furrows from his brow by winning the Open Championship for a third time. Victory in the Scandinavian Open a couple of weeks later seemed like a lap of honour. Now, 10 years after his only

win in the German Open, he needed another success to complete a hat-trick on the Volvo Tour.

Winning tournaments, if we are to respect the view of golf's master-craftsmen, comes down to the last nine holes. If that is true it was apparent by then that Jimmy Heggarty, the former Irish amateur international, and Australian Mike Harwood, who together shared the first round lead, were not going to triumph. The same applied to another Australian, Wayne Riley, and the American Bob E. Smith. They were not about to improve on the scores of 67 which had carried them into a halfway tie with Harwood.

Bernhard Langer, too, had about as much chance of winning his fifth German Open title as Maurice Flitcroft does of getting into Europe's Ryder Cup team. Yet they both share a common attribute — neither knows when to quit. So Langer, despite the putting yips, manfully shrugged off an aura of

despair to complete all 72-holes, albeit a distance behind Ballesteros.

If the Spaniard feared anyone on German soil it had to be Langer. Their respect for each other is colossal. Langer had long ago lost his fear of Ballesteros but now, with their hero banished to the shadows by his putting, the West German press seized upon Ballesteros on the eve of the final round.

Did he not feel that he would intimidate his rivals into submission? Ballesteros glanced at the interrogator, smiled and summed-up the situation. 'Tomorrow,' he said. 'We just play golf.'

Ballesteros was wrong. He did more than just play golf. He pieced together 18 riveting holes which left the German audience spellbound. Ballesteros set out on this densely wooded course in third place with Richard Boxall two shots ahead of him and Gordon Brand Junior three ahead. Boxall perished, so did Brand.

The Spaniard can conjure sheer magic on a course, especially when nothing is interfering with his concentration. Even when he backed into Ian Wright, his caddie of only four months, he was unmoved. Smiling, Ballesteros joked: 'Hey, who do you think you're working for — Bob Charles?' They laughed together and the cameras snapped. Ballesteros gave them a fair time then said: 'That's enough, please. This is a golf tournament, not a zoo.'

True, of course, but Brand must have felt he was being stalked. At the fifth Ballesteros had come out of a bunker to within a foot for a birdie four. He extracted another birdie from the sixth and, following all the humour on the tee, made a two at the 197-yards seventh where he struck a three iron to

Blasts from Peter Baker and Bernhard Langer

Richard Boxall

10 feet from the hole. He was out in 32, three under par, compared to Brand's 34 and level with his rival after a 12-foot putt gave him another two at the 11th.

Brand would contribute to his own downfall by taking six at the 424-yard 13th hole. In effect it mattered not. By then Ballesteros was totally in command and he knew it. He picked up five shots on par over the last five holes with three birdies and an eagle three at the 495-yard 17th where he charged home a putt of 40 feet.

No story about a tournament would be complete without a fairy tale or two. So as Brand held on to second place, five shots behind the winner, the spotlight swung first onto Bill Longmuir and then onto Colin Montgomerie. Longmuir entered the event in 122nd place in the Volvo Order of Merit with £8,336. He went home £15,956 richer and in 66th place, after a closing 64 placed him joint third. Montgomerie, another Scot without the accent to prove it, secured a place in his natural team in the Dunhill Cup at St Andrews in only his ninth month as a professional. He did so by achieving the top-32 finish he required to edge out Sam Torrance.

Yet the star of the show still had the last word over the supporting cast. On the last green caddie Wright reminded his employer that there was a Rolex watch on offer for the lowest round of the championship. Wright alerted Ballesteros: 'You've got this putt to win me the watch.' Seve smiled, looked at the 22-foot putt and said: 'Give me the correct line and the watch is yours'

Wright studied the line and told his man to hit it on the left lip. Ballesteros was as true with the putt as he was with his word. It gave him a winning 21 under par aggregate of 263 and Wright the watch. But who would want to be in Wright's shoes if he ever arrives late for a Ballesteros tee-off time?

Gordon Brand Jr

All smiles from the winner

POS	NAME	CTRY	1	2	3	4	TOTAL	PRIZE MONEY
1	Seve BALLESTEROS	Sp	68	68	65	62	263	£47244
2	Gordon BRAND Jr	Scot	67	69	62	70	268	£31464
3	Mike CLAYTON	Aus	68	68	68	65	269	£15959
	Bill LONGMUIR	Scot	71	67	67	64	269	£15959
5	Mark JAMES	Eng	71	69	65	65	270	£12000
6	Richard BOXALL	Eng	68	69	62	72	271	£7965
	Des SMYTH	Ire	66	69	69	67	271	£7965
	Carl MASON	Eng	67	71	66	67	271	£7965
	Bob E SMITH	USA	67	67	69	68	271	£7965
10	Peter SENIOR	Aus	67	69	66	70	272	£5253
	Frank NOBILO	NZ	67	68	69	68	272	£5253
	Mike SMITH	USA	71	66	67	68	272	£5253
13	Craig PARRY	Aus	67	71	67	68	273	£4266
	Jeff HAWKES	SA	68	70	71	64	273	£4266
	Denis DURNIAN	Eng	67	70	65	71	273	£4266
	Bryan NORTON	USA	70	65	71	67	273	£4266
17	Philip WALTON	Ire	71	70	70	63	274	£3394
	Jimmy HEGGARTY	N.Ire	65	70	69	70	274	£3394
	Eamonn DARCY	Ire	66	69	68	71	274	£3394
	Ronan RAFFERTY	N.Ire	71	68	68	67	274	£3394
	Tony CHARNLEY	Eng	69	70	67	68	274	£3394
	Mark ROE	Eng	70	69	68	67	274	£3394
	Brett OGLE	Aus	66	70	69	69	274	£3394
25	John BLAND	SA	70	69	67	69	275	£2848
	Colin MONTGOMERIE	Scot	69	70	66	70	275	£2848
	Tony JOHNSTONE	Zim	71	70	70	64	275	£2848
	Mark MCNULTY	Zim	69	72	64	70	275	£2848
29	Mike HARWOOD	Aus	65	69	68	74	276	£2551
	Bernhard LANGER	W.Ger	72	67	68	69	276	£2551
	Andrew OLDCORN	Eng	69	71	67	69	276	£2551
32	Paul CURRY	Eng	69	73	68	67	277	£2352
	Vicente FERNANDEZ	Arg	70	70	71	66	277	£2352
34	Gavin LEVENSON	SA	73	69	69	67	278	£2182
	Juan ANGLADA	Sp	69	71	68	70	278	£2182
	Manuel PINERO	Sp	70	71	69	68	278	£2182
	Teddy WEBBER	Zim	74	68	69	67	278	£2182
38	Christy O'CONNOR Jr	Ire	66	70	70	73	279	£1984
	Howard CLARK	Eng	69	69	74	67	279	£1984
	Stephen BENNETT	Eng	68	72	70	69	279	£1984
41	John SLAUGHTER	USA	67	70	69	74	280	£1644
	David A RUSSELL	Eng	70	70	73	67	280	£1644
	Manuel CALERO	Sp	71	71	70	68	280	£1644
	Martin POXON	Eng	72	69	71	68	280	£1644
	John MORGAN	Eng	71	70	70	69	280	£1644
	Andrew MURRAY	Eng	69	71	69	71	280	£1644
	Andrew SHERBORNE	Eng	67	74	71	68	280	£1644
	Chris MOODY	Eng	72	68	71	69	280	£1644
	Peter MITCHELL	Eng	72	69	72	67	280	£1644
50	Jerry HAAS	USA	69	73	69	70	281	£1162
	Jim RUTLEDGE	Can	70	71	74	66	281	£1162
	Ronald STELTEN	USA	68	74	68	71	281	£1162
	Philip HARRISON	Eng	72	67	72	70	281	£1162
	Bob SHEARER	Aus	68	72	69	72	281	£1162
	David WILLIAMS	Eng	68	74	73	66	281	£1162
	Michael MCLEAN	Eng	68	73	70	70	281	£1162
	Tony STEVENS	Eng	73	67	68	73	281	£1162
58	Johan RYSTROM	Swe	67	75	66	74	282	£864
	Jose-Maria CANIZARES	Sp	68	72	74	68	282	£864
	Carlo KNAUSS	W.Ger	70	72	69	71	282	£864
	John DE FOREST	USA	72	70	67	73	282	£864
62	Ross DRUMMOND	Scot	67	75	72	69	283	£751
	Oliver ECKSTEIN	W.Ger	66	75	72	70	283	£751
	Alberto BINAGHI	It	69	73	71	70	283	£751
	Antonio POSTIGLIONE	W.Ger	69	70	74	70	283	£751
66	Grant TURNER	Eng	68	72	70	74	284	£282
	Stephen MCALLISTER	Scot	71	71	75	67	284	£282
68	Paul THOMAS	Wal	70	71	71	73	285	£278
	Antonio GARRIDO	Sp	70	67	78	70	285	£278
70	Ian MOSEY	Eng	72	69	71	74	286	£273
	Mats HALLBERG	Swe	71	71	70	74	286	£273
	Mitch ADCOCK	USA	72	70	74	70	286	£273
73	Andrew CHANDLER	Eng	74	67	75	71	287	£269
74	Michael ALLEN	USA	69	73	76	73	291	£267

some of the liveliest watering holes in Crans.

Barry Lane and Nick Faldo bend to the task of repairing pitch marks

Alpine vista frames the same pair, below

Severiano Ballesteros in anguish as his putt to tie fails to drop

Damp exchange between Ballesteros and caddie Ian Wright

Parachutists drop in on the winner

POS	NAME	CTRY	1	2	3	4	TOTAL	PRIZE MONEY
1	Chris MOODY	Eng	68	68	67	65	268	£65543
2	Ian WOOSNAM	Wal	68	66	66	69	269	£29312
	Seve BALLESTEROS	Sp	65	68	68	68	269	£29312
	Anders FORSBRAND	Swe	67	71	67	64	269	£29312
5	Peter SENIOR	Aus	70	68	64	68	270	£16651
6	Ronan RAFFERTY	N.Ire	70	66	69	67	272	£13764
7	Gordon BRAND Jr	Scot	70	68	67	68	273	£9107
	David FROST	SA	70	68	72	63	273	£9107
	Jose Maria OLAZABAL	Sp	73	69	65	66	273	£9107
	Brett OGLE	Aus	73	68	65	67	273	£9107
	Nick FALDO	Eng	67	67	71	68	273	£9107
12	Mark MOULAND	Wal	68	70	72	64	274	£6221
	Philip WALTON	Ire	71	69	66	68	274	£6221
	Ian BAKER-FINCH	Aus	71	71	68	64	274	£6221
	Frank NOBILO	NZ	67	72	67	68	274	£6221
16	Carl MASON	Eng	68	71	70	66	275	£5426
	Barry LANE	Eng	67	68	70	70	275	£5426
18	David FEHERTY	N.Ire	67	74	70	65	276	£4974
	Mike HARWOOD	Aus	68	70	69	69	276	£4974
20	Jim RUTLEDGE	Can	68	71	69	69	277	£4483
	Gordon J BRAND	Eng	69	68	71	69	277	£4483
	Sandy LYLE	Scot	76	67	65	69	277	£4483
	David WILLIAMS	Eng	73	67	66	71	277	£4483
	Jose Maria CANIZARES	Sp	67	73	69	68	277	£4483
25	Jimmy HEGGARTY	N.Ire	66	72	67	73	278	£3893
	Andrew CHANDLER	Eng	70	68	70	70	278	£3893
	Ian YOUNG	Scot	73	70	69	66	278	£3893
	Antonio GARRIDO	Sp	71	71	68	68	278	£3893
	Armando SAAVEDRA	Arg	67	73	68	70	278	£3893
30	Wayne RILEY	Aus	67	73	69	70	279	£3241
	Andrew SHERBORNE	Eng	70	72	67	70	279	£3241
	Vicente FERNANDEZ	Arg	71	69	69	70	279	£3241
	Bob SHEARER	Aus	69	72	67	71	279	£3241
	Miguel MARTIN	Sp	72	70	67	70	279	£3241
	Mitch ADCOCK	USA	68	70	70	71	279	£3241
	Martin POXON	Eng	70	69	69	71	279	£3241
37	Wayne SMITH	Aus	69	71	73	67	280	£2752
	David J RUSSELL	Eng	68	71	72	69	280	£2752
	Bill MCCOLL	Scot	66	72	73	69	280	£2752
	Mark ROE	Eng	76	65	70	69	280	£2752
	Des SMYTH	Ire	69	72	69	70	280	£2752
42	Bill LONGMUIR	Scot	71	68	77	65	281	£2398
	Andrew MURRAY	Eng	70	73	70	68	281	£2398
	Eduardo ROMERO	Arg	71	68	71	71	281	£2398
	Jerry HAAS	USA	69	74	73	65	281	£2398
46	Manuel CALERO	Sp	68	75	69	70	282	£1808
	John JACOBS	USA	70	68	72	72	282	£1808
	Grant TURNER	Eng	69	74	71	68	282	£1808
	Frederic REGARD	Fr	70	71	70	71	282	£1808
	Colin MONGOMERIE	Scot	68	72	69	73	282	£1808
	Michael ALLEN	USA	71	69	68	74	282	£1808
	Ian MOSEY	Eng	74	66	69	73	282	£1808
	Jeff HAWKES	SA	70	72	73	67	282	£1808
	Jose RIVERO	Sp	73	69	72	68	282	£1808
	Rodger DAVIS	Aus	71	71	69	71	282	£1808
	Magnus SUNESSON	Swe	72	68	72	70	282	£1808
57	Tony JOHNSTONE	Zim	70	71	70	72	283	£1271
	Emmanuel DUSSART	Fr	70	72	71	70	283	£1271
	Alberto BINAGHI	It	72	67	73	71	283	£1271
60	Peter TERAVAINEN	USA	71	68	72	73	284	£1120
	Paul THOMAS	Wal	70	70	74	70	284	£1120
	Ross DRUMMOND	Scot	72	71	70	71	284	£1120
	Mark CALCAVECCHIA	USA	68	74	69	73	284	£1120
64	Keith WATERS	Eng	74	68	74	69	285	£799
	Peter MCWHINNEY	Aus	73	69	74	69	285	£799
	John BLAND	SA	70	72	72	71	285	£799
67	Michael KING	Eng	73	70	72	71	286	£391
68	Glenn RALPH	Eng	74	69	70	74	287	£389
69	Sam TORRANCE	Scot	73	70	70	75	288	£385
	Steen TINNING	Den	73	70	75	70	288	£385
	Brian EVANS	Eng	74	69	73	72	288	£385
72	Bill MALLEY	USA	74	68	72	75	289	£381

Kiss me quick!

WOOSNAM
leads the assault

IAN WOOSNAM REVELLED IN THE CONDITIONS DURING A WEEK OF BLISSFUL WEATHER AT SUNNINGDALE AND COLLECTED HIS THIRD TITLE OF THE SEASON.

f or any golfer worthy of the name, the prospect of a round over Sunningdale's Old course is one to be savoured. Laid out in that heather and pine belt to the west of London which has provided such bounty to golf, Sunningdale is a place where a player can lose himself to the game. The Old course is not overly long, measuring 6,580 yards from the championship tees but the heather-lined fairways place a great premium on accuracy and its greens contain many subtle borrows which can fox even the most accomplished putter. Given a stiff breeze swirling among the tree-tops, the par of 70 is not easily matched but on a calm, sun-drenched day then a score in 60s is there for the taking.

Thus it was that the Volvo Tour arrived at Sunningdale for the Panasonic European Open and in a summer that had been hardly worth the name, struck a seam of perfect weather in which to make substantial hay from the £300,000 prize fund.

It was the 10th anniversary of the European Open and after a chequered financial start in the early years, the event is now a massively established part of the Tour. The size of the tented village bore out the fact that it is as much a social meeting point as a golf tournament – indeed, from the depths of the village it was easy to forget that any golf was being played a few hundred yards away. Such a proliferation of hospitality is frowned on in some quarters but without the support of the companies which take units, the European Open, and many other events, would founder. The priceless advantage golf has over other sporting watering-holes is that there is no restriction on the number of people who can

come through the gate. Therefore, the allocation of tickets to the hospitality units does not prevent the public from entering.

The combination of the weather and a field which contained all but one of the big names brought the spectators out in droves and they witnessed golf of such quality that, for once, that awful alliteration 'birdie barrage' was justified. The one missing big name was that of Severiano Ballesteros who was taking a week off from one of the few European Tour events he has never won. His reason, that there were too many big-money events in succession, struck most people as somewhat odd since the rise in prize-money is one of the reasons why European golf is currently enjoying such international success. One could hardly expect the schedule to be structured so that a tournament with a large prize-fund would be followed immediately by one of lesser value.

Whatever Ballesteros' reasons for not being at Sunningdale, it is a matter for conjecture whether he would have

improved on the rash of low scores which pervaded the score boards. In such conditions, it must be said that the par for the professionals was around 67 or 68 since both par five holes, the first and 14th were in easy reach and two of the par fours, the third and the ninth were driveable.

On the first day it was 38-year old Denis Durnian from Manchester who set the pace with a 64. Durnian is well used to being among the lower numbers since it was he who set a new record for nine holes in the Open Championship when he carded a 28 at Royal Birkdale in 1983. There was no 28 this time but he did cover the inward half in 31 and having started at 7.20 am was back in the clubhouse for a mid-morning coffee.

Hard on his heels came the trio of Jose-Maria Olazabal, Gordon Brand Junior and Ian Woosnam, all one stroke behind. Olazabal and Brand both had a touch of 'flu and the Spaniard was forced to wear a sweater in the heat to ease the shivers which racked him. There was an air of inevitability about Woosnam's round as he cruised to the turn in 31. Coming home he had the best chance of catching Durnian until he slipped a stroke at the difficult short 15th. Nick Faldo was still in the groove that had made him the Tour's most consistent performer throughout the season but his 66 could have been so much better had he holed the putts his approaches had set up for him.

Anyone around or over par had left themselves a great deal of ground to make up and in this respect, Bernhard Langer was virtually out of the tournament as his putting troubles continued to mount en route to a 75.

The emerging force of Ian Woosnam

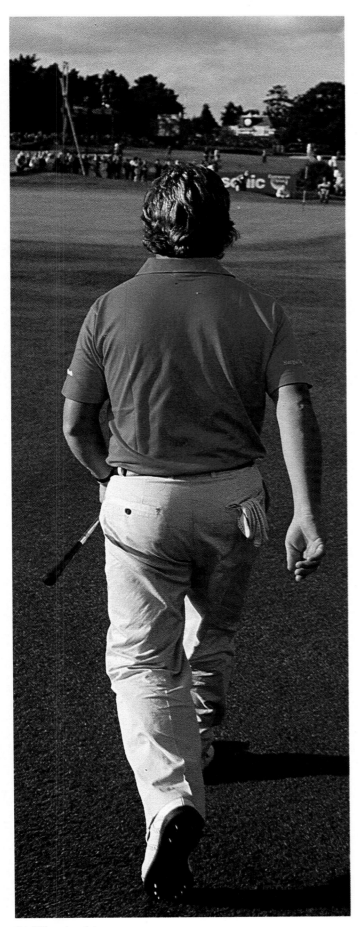

Striding to victory

POS	NAME	CTRY	1	2	3	4	TOTAL	PRIZE MONEY
1	Ian WOOSNAM	Wal	65	66	64	65	260	£50000
2	Nick FALDO	Eng	66	65	66	66	263	£33300
3	Jose Maria OLAZABAL	Sp	65	70	64	67	266	£15493
	Sandy LYLE	Scot	69	65	67	65	266	£15493
	Mark JAMES	Eng	66	70	63	67	266	£15493
6	Gordon BRAND Jr	Scot	65	70	67	65	267	£10500
7	Craig PARRY	Aus	68	70	67	63	268	£9000
8	Jose RIVERO	Sp	68	65	66	70	269	£7500
9	Brett OGLE	Aus	71	68	66	65	270	£6360
	Peter BAKER	Eng	67	68	66	69	270	£6360
11	Denis DURNIAN	Eng	64	67	69	71	271	£5170
	Mark MCNULTY	Zim	67	66	70	68	271	£5170
	Mats LANNER	Swe	68	63	69	71	271	£5170
14	Ronan RAFFERTY	N.Ire	67	74	64	67	272	£4410
	Mike HARWOOD	Aus	66	67	70	69	272	£4410
	David WILLIAMS	Eng	68	68	64	72	272	£4410
17	Teddy WEBBER	Zim	67	71	68	67	273	£3642
	Jose-Maria CANIZARES	Sp	70	69	66	68	273	£3642
	Michael KING	Eng	71	66	67	69	273	£3642
	Tony CHARNLEY	Eng	68	70	67	68	273	£3642
	Mike SMITH	USA	72	68	65	68	273	£3642
	John BLAND	SA	67	68	63	75	273	£3642
	Eduardo ROMERO	Arg	70	68	66	69	273	£3642
24	Christy O'CONNOR Jr	Ire	68	64	70	72	274	£3195
	Jerry HAAS	USA	69	66	71	68	274	£3195
26	Frank NOBILO	NZ	69	70	70	66	275	£2925
	Stephen BENNETT	Eng	71	67	66	71	275	£2925
	Peter MITCHELL	Eng	72	67	66	70	275	£2925
	Barry LANE	Eng	66	74	68	67	275	£2925
30	Mike CLAYTON	Aus	66	70	70	70	276	£2538
	Noel RATCLIFFE	Aus	67	73	67	69	276	£2538
	Richard BOXALL	Eng	66	71	67	72	276	£2538
	Carl MASON	Eng	70	70	64	72	276	£2538
	Bill MAYFAIR	USA	66	72	69	69	276	£2538
35	Rodger DAVIS	Aus	70	71	68	68	277	£2160
	Andrew SHERBORNE	Eng	73	67	70	67	277	£2160
	Philip WALTON	Ire	69	71	69	68	277	£2160
	Gordon J BRAND	Eng	70	71	67	69	277	£2160
	Roger CHAPMAN	Eng	69	66	72	70	277	£2160
	Jeff HAWKES	SA	69	66	71	71	277	£2160
	Wayne RILEY	Aus	68	67	69	73	277	£2160
42	Santiago LUNA	Sp	70	68	70	70	278	£1830
	Ross DRUMMOND	Scot	70	69	70	69	278	£1830
	John JACOBS	USA	71	70	71	66	278	£1830
	Andrew MURRAY	Eng	69	71	68	70	278	£1830
46	Magnus JONSSON	Swe	71	65	71	72	279	£1530
	Neal BRIGGS	Eng	72	67	67	73	279	£1530
	Ossie MOORE	Aus	70	68	69	72	279	£1530
	Ian YOUNG	Scot	67	66	74	72	279	£1530
	Gary KOCH	USA	68	71	69	71	279	£1530
	Bob SHEARER	Aus	70	70	69	70	279	£1530
52	Ronald STELTEN	USA	67	69	74	70	280	£1260
	Hugh BAIOCCHI	SA	68	68	75	69	280	£1260
	Miguel MARTIN	Sp	71	70	69	70	280	£1260
55	Paul CURRY	Eng	71	70	70	70	281	£1110
	Vaughan SOMERS	Aus	71	70	66	74	281	£1110
57	John DE FOREST	USA	70	70	72	70	282	£904
	Bernard GALLACHER	Scot	69	71	69	73	282	£904
	Jim RUTLEDGE	Can	71	70	69	72	282	£904
	Magnus SUNESSON	Swe	71	66	68	77	282	£904
	Chris MOODY	Eng	73	68	71	70	282	£904
	Mats HALLBERG	Swe	67	71	73	71	282	£904
	Howard CLARK	Eng	71	69	75	67	282	£904
64	Bryan NORTON	USA	69	69	72	73	283	£610
	Andrew CHANDLER	Eng	68	68	73	74	283	£610
	Grant TURNER	Eng	69	70	72	72	283	£610
67	Armando SAAVEDRA	Arg	70	71	74	69	284	£297
	Emmanuel DUSSART	Fr	74	67	68	75	284	£297
69	Ove SELLBERG	Swe	70	67	76	72	285	£293
	Jimmy HEGGARTY	N.Ire	72	69	76	68	285	£293
71	Bob E SMITH	USA	69	70	75	72	286	£290
72	Mitch ADCOCK	USA	73	68	78	68	287	£288
73	Jeff HALL	Eng	70	71	76	74	291	£286

HURRICANE
Seve hits Paris

*t*hey flew to France, the top 50 players in Europe and some imported Americans, in pursuit of the second largest purse of the season. It wasn't Paris in spring time but Paris in autumn with £400,000 on offer was a more than adequate substitute.

What drew them all was the 19th staging of the Trophée Lancôme, which meant the 19th year of those striking posters and the 19th year of returning to the fabulous clubhouse at St Nom la Breteche, once a farm for the Palace of Versailles and later the headquarters for the invading Germans. For 19 years the ducks have squawked on the pond between the putting green and the first tee and spectacularly-dressed Parisians have strutted around the course like peacocks in full plumage. In all that time not a match has left the first tee without each player being introduced at great length by Patrice Galitzine, a white Russian descendent.

Since Tony Jacklin first won this bizarre trophy in 1970 – it is a bas relief of the male torso with a golf ball in the heart – few players have taken such a grip on it as Seve Ballesteros did this time. It's easy to say, after his first nine holes of 18 strokes and 12 putts gave him a seven under par 64 and a lead of four strokes, that he was always going to win. He coasted home easily after rounds that went up in almost mathematical progression and left Jose-Maria Olazabal, Sandy Lyle and Greg Norman, among others, sprawling in his wake.

With this victory Ballesteros sent everyone scurrying to the record books to discover that since the beginning of July his performances have been astonishing: played in six events in Europe, won four of them and came

THE BRILLIANCE OF BALLESTEROS OUTSHONE HIS RIVALS ONCE AGAIN. ONLY THIS TIME HIS TRIUMPH AT ST NOM LA BRETECHE PLACED HIM IN AN INVINCIBLE POSITION AT THE TOP OF THE MONEY-WINNERS' LIST.

second in one other. He was 124 under par for 12 tournaments in Europe this season. His stroke average was 68.43 and he failed to beat par in only two of his last 24 rounds. This was golf of the highest order, probably as good as anyone in the world has ever played for a comparable period, taking into account the weather and the severity of the courses.

Little wonder then that victory in Paris all but assured Ballesteros of the leading position in the 1988 Volvo Order of Merit. By the time Seve's £66,600 from Paris was included he had won £353,384 from this tumultuous season and no one else had a realistic chance of getting near him. The closest was Nick Faldo and he was nearly £100,000 behind.

For Faldo it was a situation he had become used to. He too was having an astonishing run in tournaments. Since mid-May, he had played 13 events in Europe and the US, compiling a stroke

average of 68.96. He finished outside the top 10 once – 54th at Westchester on the eve of the US Open in June – and his one victory had come in the French Open in the week after the US Open. Of the remaining 11 events he had finished second in six, most recently the Sunday before the Lancôme when a 17 under par total around Sunningdale was only good enough to get him within three strokes of Ian Woosnam. Prior to arriving in Paris, he had been second in three of his last five events.

What was wrong with Faldo was his putting. Two years ago to have said Faldo couldn't putt would have been as improbable as saying Hercules wasn't strong. But these days Faldo is mortal on the greens. He looks less comfortable over the ball. He fidgets. He three putts. He misses putts in the five to 15 feet range he once would have holed. He is, in short, a shadow of himself.

He spent hours on the putting green in Paris, oblivious to the squawking ducks, marking out a line with blue chalk and then checking that his stroke followed the prescribed line. His faithful caddie Andy Prodger checked his boss's aim, alignment, sometimes even held Faldo's head to prevent it moving. Nothing was left to chance. It was to no avail however and a visibly tired Faldo slumped to tie 28th.

Another player with putting problems – but much more severe than Faldo's – was Langer and it wasn't until the fourth round that he got some respite from the agony he has been through on the greens recently. His 68, 11 shots better than his opening round, contained six birdies in his last eight holes and may have been a harbinger of better things to come. There are many things you might wish on a man; the yips are not one of them.

It was left to Lyle, who set a new course record in the second round; to Olazabal, the only player to record four sub-70 rounds; to Greg Norman, thanks to a late burst; and to Ronan Rafferty, who equalled Lyle's 63 on the last day, to draw close to Ballesteros — and it wasn't very close.

No one was going to get close enough to worry him. His main worry was himself and how to maintain his concentration while he, Lyle and Olazabal were held up on almost every shot by the South African trio of Jeff

Ballesteros stretched
away from the field

Hawkes, Mark McNulty and John Bland. On the ninth tee Ballesteros could stand it no more and he complained to a PGA official who passed on the Spaniard's feelings to the trio in front. There were no more hold-ups.

Ballesteros won by four shots, his fifth victory of the year in Europe, his sixth world-wide. It is surely his finest year and one had visions of French golf enthusiasts going in their separate ways from St Nom la Breteche and one after the other remarking: 'Pardon monsieur, avez-vous vu le cyclone Seve?'.

Le parc du golf
St Nom

Big four at the finish. Above,
Greg Norman and Sandy Lyle; below,
Severiano Ballesteros and
Jose-Maria Olazabal

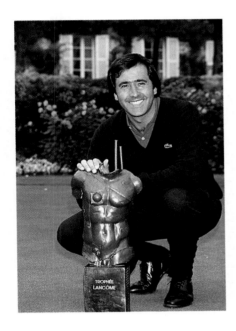

A week when the winner watched a lot of birdies, thanked his caddie and collected golf's most bizarre trophy

POS	NAME	CTRY	1	2	3	4	TOTAL	PRIZE MONEY
1	Seve BALLESTEROS	Sp	64	66	68	71	269	£66660
2	Jose Maria OLAZABAL	Sp	69	66	69	69	273	£44400
3	Greg NORMAN	Aus	71	72	68	67	278	£22520
	Sandy LYLE	Scot	75	63	68	72	278	£22520
5	Ronan RAFFERTY	N.Ire	71	70	75	63	279	£16940
6	Rodger DAVIS	Aus	71	73	71	65	280	£14000
7	Jose RIVERO	Sp	74	68	69	70	281	£8220
	Peter BAKER	Eng	70	67	74	70	281	£8220
	Chris MOODY	Eng	71	68	72	70	281	£8220
	John BLAND	SA	71	69	69	72	281	£8220
	Christy O'CONNOR Jr	Ire	72	72	70	67	281	£8220
	Tony JOHNSTONE	Zim	74	71	67	69	281	£8220
	Richard BOXALL	Eng	70	77	69	65	281	£8220
	Jeff HAWKES	SA	75	68	67	71	281	£8220
15	Marc PENDARIES	Fr	69	76	69	68	282	£5520
	Mark JAMES	Eng	68	72	72	70	282	£5520
	Eamonn DARCY	Ire	72	68	72	70	282	£5520
	David FEHERTY	N.Ire	72	71	71	68	282	£5520
19	Mark MOULAND	Wal	72	70	71	70	283	£4688
	Carl MASON	Eng	75	73	70	65	283	£4688
	Sam TORRANCE	Scot	71	68	71	73	283	£4688
	Denis DURNIAN	Eng	70	70	72	71	283	£4688
	Gordon J BRAND	Eng	70	73	69	71	283	£4688
24	Miguel MARTIN	Sp	70	73	71	70	284	£4140
	Tony CHARNLEY	Eng	75	67	70	72	284	£4140
	Mark ROE	Eng	72	72	70	70	284	£4140
	Ian WOOSNAM	Wal	69	74	69	72	284	£4140
28	Jim THORPE	USA	73	67	70	75	285	£3600
	Philip WALTON	Ire	72	71	75	67	285	£3600
	Andrew MURRAY	Eng	72	72	69	72	285	£3600
	Gordon BRAND Jr	Scot	72	70	71	72	285	£3600
	Nick FALDO	Eng	72	72	73	68	285	£3600
33	Roger CHAPMAN	Eng	69	77	69	71	286	£3160
	Frank NOBILO	NZ	71	71	71	73	286	£3160
	Michael ALLEN	USA	70	74	73	69	286	£3160
	Howard CLARK	Eng	72	72	67	75	286	£3160
37	Craig PARRY	Aus	68	71	72	76	287	£2760
	Frederic REGARD	Fr	73	70	74	70	287	£2760
	Eduardo ROMERO	Arg	74	74	69	70	287	£2760
	Mark MCNULTY	Zim	74	64	70	79	287	£2760
	Peter SENIOR	Aus	72	74	72	69	287	£2760
	Mike CLAYTON	Aus	74	67	75	71	287	£2760
43	Stephen BENNETT	Eng	73	70	74	71	288	£2280
	Jim RUTLEDGE	Can	74	75	71	68	288	£2280
	Jose Maria CANIZARES	Sp	72	71	70	75	288	£2280
	David WILLIAMS	Eng	73	71	73	71	288	£2280
	Derrick COOPER	Eng	74	71	69	74	288	£2280
	David WHELAN	Eng	71	75	68	74	288	£2280
49	David J RUSSELL	Eng	69	76	74	71	290	£2000
50	Mike HARWOOD	Aus	75	71	69	76	291	£1840
	Colin MONTGOMERIE	Scot	70	72	76	73	291	£1840
	Des SMYTH	Ire	71	73	72	75	291	£1840
53	Vicente FERNANDEZ	Arg	76	71	72	73	292	£1680
54	Bernhard LANGER	W.Ger	79	73	73	68	293	£1560
	David LLEWELLYN	Wal	72	74	74	73	293	£1560
56	Hugh BAIOCCHI	SA	74	72	74	74	294	£1440
57	Manuel PINERO	Sp	78	72	72	73	295	£1320
	Mike SMITH	USA	77	74	73	71	295	£1320
59	Paul WAY	Eng	71	76	75	74	296	£1220
	Barry LANE	Eng	77	74	72	73	296	£1220
61	John MORGAN	Eng	74	74	74	76	298	£1160
62	Anders FORSBRAND	Swe	70	77	80	73	300	£1120
63	Robert LEE	Eng	82	72	74	81	309	£1040
	Wayne RILEY	Aus	77	80	74	78	309	£1040
	Peter FOWLER	Aus	80	79	72	78	309	£1040
66	Emmanuel DUSSART	Fr	76	77	RETD			£1000

prematurely than others – and Langer could not sustain his deliverance, following with rounds of 75, 71 and 79 littered with the dreaded 'yips.'

The first day's honours went to a 40-year-old wedge, wielded with magical effect by Eamonn Darcy who transformed potential disaster into a glorious 66 after holing a 95-yard pitch at the ninth for an eagle two. Darcy confessed to be labouring towards the end of a long, hard season but his spirits were revived by a 16-year-old putter, once rejected by Seve Ballesteros. The Irishman had only 12 putts in the last 10 holes to post a six under par early on a warm September day.

Darcy revealed: 'I found the wedge in an oddments bin in a Singapore club shop 10 years ago and it has been with me ever since. I've had my putter since I joined the tour in 1971. Seve borrowed it for two months and gave it back – I'm glad he did.' Darcy, however, added 10 shots to his score on the second day in a troublesome crosswind which blew throughout the rest of the tournament.

Seve sent sparks flying with a chip-in eagle three at the 14th via overhead power cables crossing the fairway as he moved to a 70, while Smyth (68) scored the 10th ace of his career at the fifth hole to share the halfway lead with Lanner (70). The Irish-Swedish partnership blossomed again on the third day but their jubilation was muted when Ballesteros joined them on a six below par 210. Smyth, awarded the tortuous task of accompanying the Open Champion during the final round, battled gamely to a 71 to finish runner-up for a third time this season alongside Forsbrand, who scuttled through the pack with a 68.

Olazabal avenged two earlier defeats by Ballesteros, who ultimately finished joint sixth but enhanced his reputation as a gentleman as well as the most gifted scholar of modern times.

Trouble hangs over Bernhard Langer on the 14th during the last round

All the signs point to star status for Olazabal

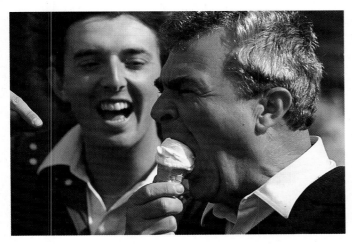

Cold comfort for Sandy Lyle's caddie, Dave Musgrove

Here's looking at you, kid. Caddie and winner share the moment

POS	NAME	CTRY	1	2	3	4	TOTAL	PRIZE MONEY
1	Jose Maria OLAZABAL	Sp	69	72	70	68	279	£47770
2	Anders FORSBRAND	Swe	75	68	70	68	281	£24878
	Des SMYTH	Ire	71	68	71	71	281	£24878
4	Tom PURTZER	USA	68	72	72	70	282	£13232
	Mark MCNULTY	Zim	69	72	71	70	282	£13232
6	Ronan RAFFERTY	N.Ire	75	69	72	68	284	£9315
	Seve BALLESTEROS	Sp	72	70	68	74	284	£9315
8	Jeff HAWKES	SA	78	70	69	68	285	£6793
	Jose RIVERO	Sp	71	71	72	71	285	£6793
10	Philip WALTON	Ire	70	71	75	70	286	£5503
	Mats LANNER	Swe	69	70	71	76	286	£5503
12	Eamonn DARCY	Ire	66	76	71	74	287	£4772
	Nick FALDO	Eng	73	71	72	71	287	£4772
14	Sandy LYLE	Scot	69	75	72	72	288	£4213
	David FEHERTY	N.Ire	73	69	70	76	288	£4213
	Ian MOSEY	Eng	70	72	72	74	288	£4213
17	Jerry ANDERSON	Can	71	72	70	76	289	£3707
	Ian WOOSNAM	Wal	72	70	73	74	289	£3707
	Paul WAY	Eng	74	72	72	71	289	£3707
20	Miguel MARTIN	Sp	75	71	70	74	290	£3396
	Sam TORRANCE	Scot	74	71	71	74	290	£3396
22	Denis DURNIAN	Eng	71	74	74	72	291	£3181
	Juan ANGLADA	Sp	73	69	73	76	291	£3181
	Mark ROE	Eng	67	75	71	78	291	£3181
25	Gordon J BRAND	Eng	68	76	75	73	292	£2794
	Andrew OLDCORN	Eng	74	70	74	74	292	£2794
	John SLAUGHTER	USA	70	72	74	76	292	£2794
	Robert LEE	Eng	76	72	75	69	292	£2794
	Malcolm MACKENZIE	Eng	73	74	75	70	292	£2794
	Paul THOMAS	Wal	76	71	74	71	292	£2794
31	David JONES	N.Ire	72	72	71	78	293	£2417
	Peter TERAVAINEN	USA	71	73	74	75	293	£2417
	Bernhard LANGER	W.Ger	68	75	71	79	293	£2417
34	Carl MASON	Eng	74	72	72	76	294	£2178
	Bernard GALLACHER	Scot	75	72	74	73	294	£2178
	Gordon BRAND Jr	Scot	76	73	70	75	294	£2178
	Andrew MURRAY	Eng	74	71	77	72	294	£2178
	Jim RUTLEDGE	Can	70	75	75	74	294	£2178
39	Ian YOUNG	Scot	71	73	76	75	295	£1891
	Carlo KNAUSS	W.Ger	74	72	76	73	295	£1891
	Antonio POSTIGLIONE	W.Ger	74	73	75	73	295	£1891
	Magnus PERSSON	Swe	70	73	74	78	295	£1891
	Peter BAKER	Eng	77	70	74	74	295	£1891
44	Chris MOODY	Eng	73	73	76	74	296	£1633
	David A RUSSELL	Eng	75	73	75	73	296	£1633
	Andrew SHERBORNE	Eng	71	75	75	75	296	£1633
	Magnus SUNESSON	Swe	74	72	78	72	296	£1633
48	Emmanuel DUSSART	Fr	73	76	77	71	297	£1318
	Ove SELLBERG	Swe	74	71	75	77	297	£1318
	Derrick COOPER	Eng	71	78	75	73	297	£1318
	Manuel PINERO	Sp	71	75	75	76	297	£1318
	Christy O'CONNOR Jr	Ire	74	75	78	70	297	£1318
	Torsten GIEDEON	W.Ger	76	73	74	74	297	£1318
	Steen TINNING	Den	75	72	75	75	297	£1318
55	Manuel CALERO	Sp	72	75	77	74	298	£960
	Roger CHAPMAN	Eng	72	75	76	75	298	£960
	Michael KING	Eng	73	75	76	75	298	£960
	Tony JOHNSTONE	Zim	76	71	74	77	298	£960
	John MORGAN	Eng	72	74	76	76	298	£960
	Glenn RALPH	Eng	71	75	74	78	298	£960
61	Frederic REGARD	Fr	74	74	74	77	299	£816
	Stephen BENNETT	Eng	74	71	79	75	299	£816
63	Santiago LUNA	Sp	79	70	73	78	300	£773
	Sven STRUEVER	W.Ger	73	76	76	75	300	(AM)
64	Emilio RODRIGUEZ	Sp	76	73	76	76	301	£508
	Keith WATERS	Eng	72	76	75	78	301	£508
	Brian MARCHBANK	Scot	73	76	76	76	301	£508
	Thomas GOEGELE	W.Ger	75	73	75	78	301	£508
	Hans-Gunter REITER	W.Ger	77	72	77	78	304	(AM)
68	Vaughan SOMERS	Aus	70	77	85	73	305	£283
69	Paul CURRY	Eng	74	75	81	76	306	£281
70	Martin POXON	Eng	74	75	DIS		149	£279

CLARK'S
lean spell ends early

When Howard Clark decided to follow Nick Faldo's example — and gamble — by making considerable technical changes to his widely-acclaimed golf swing, he prepared himself for a couple of lean years.

Ten major tournament wins in the space of 10 years is a considerable record but Clark has always aimed for golf's ultimate prize, the Open Championship. Thus it was he consulted golf's modern guru, the British-born, Florida-based David Leadbetter. Clark told his close friends: 'I don't think I can win the Open with my present swing. Changing is a gamble but I can afford it and I'm prepared to take it. I'm also prepared to be patient.'

For most of the season, Clark did not have many opportunities to put his new method to the test of playing under pressure but his chance came in the first English Open at Royal Birkdale.

The idea for an English Open was conceived jointly by Yorkshire-based tournament promoters, EGP Sports Group and PGA European Tour Enterprises. Sponsorship talks with a leading British company were well advanced when, for reasons beyond that company's control, the arrangements fell through. Despite valiant efforts by both organisations, it became apparent that big companies were not geared to re-arranging their budgets and marketing programmes at such short notice. But at no time was there any suggestion that the tournament should be shelved until proper backing could be found. Both Gerry Connolly, chairman of EGP, and George O'Grady, managing director of PGA European Tour Enterprises, are men of vision and they decided, without hesitation, to underwrite the

IN THE MIDDLE OF RE-STRUCTURING HIS SWING HOWARD CLARK CAST ASIDE ANY DOUBTS REGARDING THE WISDOM OF HIS DECISION BY WINNING THE INAUGURAL ENGLISH OPEN AT ROYAL BIRKDALE.

costs of the event as an investment for the future.

It was a brave decision and, being staged on one of the world's finest golf courses, Royal Birkdale, it was hoped that most of the leading players would give the inaugural event their support. Sadly, most of them by-passed a chance at the £180,000 prize fund, preferring to take a rest between a string of richer tournaments.

In a somewhat weakened field the powerful Clark was a clear favourite, although such a thought had not crossed his mind until a casual comment in the competitors' car park on the morning of the first round. 'The organisers are delighted that you're playing this week when some of the other top players are missing,' Clark was told.

The remark struck home. 'It was the nicest thing anybody had said to me for a long time,' recalled Clark. 'I said to myself, I'd better get stuck in here and

do something.' He stepped onto the first tee an hour later with only one thought in his mind — victory. But would his new swing, still very much at the experimental stage, stand up to being in contention for a title?

Some of the less well known names took the opportunity to claim a little instant stardom by taking up the running on an exceptionally difficult first day played in near gale force winds. David Ray, who had missed the cut in his previous 11 tournaments, shared the first round lead on 70 with Paul Curry and Magnus Persson but after that it was the established players who took over.

Des Smyth, with seven runner-up finishes under his belt during the season, was looking to break that run and he set about the task in fine style. He came to the last hole in the second round needing a par four for a nine under par 63 but fluffed a delicate chip shot into a greenside bunker and took six. Every watching golf fan knew how he felt and Smyth put a brave face on it all afterwards by saying. 'It was a disappointing end to what was nearly a perfect round of golf. I must have been a bit anxious on that chip shot because I just duffed it into the bunker. Chipping is normally a strong part of my game.'

Nevertheless, a seven under par 65 at Royal Birkdale is pretty good and Smyth took over the lead. He was still up there after a 70 in the third round, one stroke ahead of Clark.

Peter Baker, winner of the Benson and Hedges title at Fulford, provided the main challenge in the final round, played in perfect sunny weather. He pitched into the battle for the £30,000 first prize with seven birdies, but he also fell foul of Birkdale's hidden terrors and never put undue pressure on Clark,

POS	NAME	CTRY	1	2	3	4	TOTAL	PRIZE MONEY
1	Howard CLARK	Eng	72	71	67	69	279	£30000
2	Peter BAKER	Eng	73	70	69	70	282	£20000
3	Des SMYTH	Ire	74	65	70	74	283	£10150
	Peter MCWHINNEY	Aus	75	67	74	67	283	£10150
5	Stephen MCALLISTER	Scot	73	69	73	69	284	£7000
	Miguel MARTIN	Sp	74	71	72	67	284	£7000
7	David J RUSSELL	Eng	74	70	70	71	285	£5400
8	Tony CHARNLEY	Eng	74	73	69	70	286	£4130
	Bill LONGMUIR	Scot	74	70	72	70	286	£4130
10	Richard BOXALL	Eng	74	71	76	66	287	£3300
	Mark MOULAND	Wal	75	73	70	69	287	£3300
13	Martin POXON	Eng	76	70	72	70	288	£2575
	Bernard GALLACHER	Scot	72	73	72	71	288	£2575
	Marc PENDARIES	Fr	74	74	72	68	288	£2575
	Andrew MURRAY	Eng	79	70	70	69	288	£2575
	Derrick COOPER	Eng	74	73	71	70	288	£2575
	Chris MOODY	Eng	72	68	72	76	288	£2575
	Philip WALTON	Ire	77	69	71	71	288	£2575
	Andrew SHERBORNE	Eng	72	74	69	73	288	£2575
21	David FEHERTY	N.Ire	76	70	75	68	289	£2040
	Paul CURRY	Eng	70	74	74	71	289	£2040
	Peter FOWLER	Aus	71	77	71	70	289	£2040
	Ian MOSEY	Eng	75	71	71	72	289	£2040
	David A RUSSELL	Eng	73	71	74	71	289	£2040
26	Roger CHAPMAN	Eng	75	68	76	71	290	£1645
	Denis DURNIAN	Eng	76	71	72	71	290	£1645
	Michael MCLEAN	Eng	73	73	73	71	290	£1645
	Gordon J BRAND	Eng	74	72	73	71	290	£1645
	Brian WAITES	Eng	76	73	71	70	290	£1645
	Gordon BRAND Jr	Scot	74	69	77	70	290	£1645
	Russell WEIR	Scot	74	68	74	74	290	£1645
33	Peter MITCHELL	Eng	75	73	71	72	291	£1440
	David RAY	Eng	70	77	73	71	291	£1440
	Philip HARRISON	Eng	73	73	71	74	291	£1440
36	Jerry ANDERSON	Can	74	73	76	69	292	£1260
	Kyi Hla HAN	Bur	73	72	78	69	292	£1260
	Andrew CHANDLER	Eng	72	73	74	73	292	£1260
	David WILLIAMS	Eng	74	68	78	72	292	£1260
	Magnus PERSSON	Swe	70	75	79	68	292	£1260
	Mark ROE	Eng	76	72	72	72	292	£1260
43	Andrew OLDCORN	Eng	78	71	72	72	293	£1020
	Bryan NORTON	USA	73	71	74	75	293	£1020
	Colin MONTGOMERIE	Scot	75	72	75	71	293	£1020
	Ross DRUMMOND	Scot	77	70	76	70	293	£1020
	Paul WAY	Eng	76	71	74	72	293	£1020
	John MCHENRY	Ire	76	73	74	70	293	£1020
48	Ross MCFARLANE	Eng	76	71	74	73	294	£840
	Mike MILLER	Scot	73	70	77	74	294	£840
	Glenn RALPH	Eng	76	69	77	72	294	£840
51	Chris PLATTS	Eng	77	72	74	72	295	£740
	Alberto BINIGHI	It	76	71	76	72	295	£740
	David JONES	N.Ire	73	72	77	73	295	£740
54	Keith WATERS	Eng	76	69	75	76	296	£680
	Jeremy BENNETT	Eng	73	73	74	76	296	£680
	Brian MARCHBANK	Scot	78	69	72	77	296	£680
57	Jesper PARNEVIK	Swe	79	70	75	73	297	£640
58	Stephen HAMELL	N.Ire	79	70	75	74	298	£610
	John O'LEARY	Ire	76	73	79	70	298	£610
60	Laurie TURNER	Eng	77	70	78	74	299	£580
61	Paul HOAD	Eng	74	70	79	77	300	£520
	Jonas SAXTON	USA	75	72	80	73	300	£520
	Stephen BENNETT	Eng	71	78	78	73	300	£520
	Stuart SMITH	Eng	73	74	81	72	300	£520
	Craig LAURENCE	Eng	74	73	77	76	300	£520

Birkdale spot the ball
competition

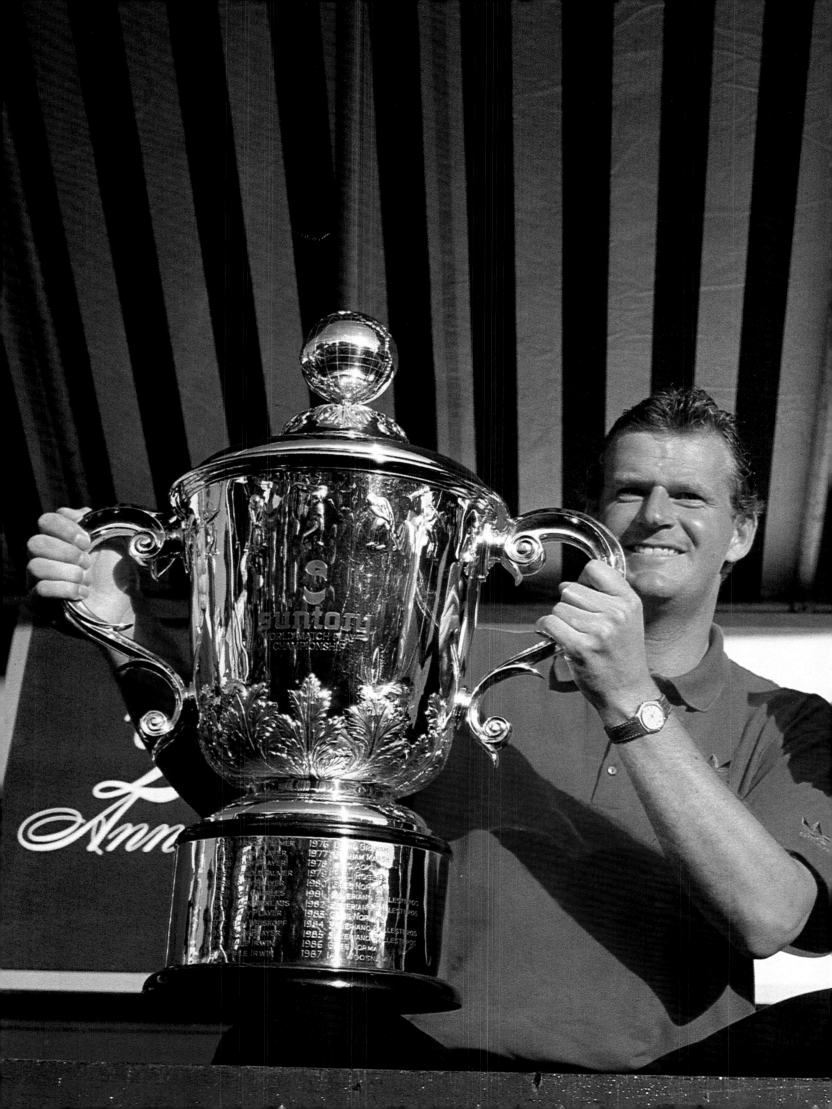

LYLE

wins it in the fifth

*t*he two club members playing over the West course on a Monday took a large crowd with them and the stakes were a little more than a pound a corner.

The 25th final of the World Match-Play Championship was taking place and club member number 273 (Sandy Lyle) was taking on club member number 2483 (Nick Faldo) in the second all-British final in a row and, for Lyle, his third successive final appearance.

Heady days indeed for British golfers, particularly as Neil Coles, runner-up to Arnold Palmer in the first Championship in 1964, remained the only British finalist until Lyle came through in 1980 before losing to Greg Norman. Then last year Ian Woosnam beat the unfortunate Lyle in a marvellous match which went to the 36th green. Lyle had also lost to Norman in 1986 and had been 'done' by Severiano Ballesteros in 1982 when the Spaniard holed a monstrous putt across a water-logged 37th green. If anyone deserved this title it was Sandy Lyle.

For Faldo, final appearances were fewer. Just the one in 1983 when Greg Norman had defeated him and in looking at his opponent this time he needed no reminding that the only other occasion they had faced each other at Wentworth, in 1982, Faldo had been six up over 18 holes only to lose two and one. In terms of purity of striking, no one in 1988 had come close to Faldo's machine-like contact but all he had to show for it was one victory and seven runner-up finishes, the most galling coming in the US Open play-off with Curtis Strange.

The two finalists had both been seeded at the beginning of the week but neither were scheduled to progress beyond the semi-finals. Their fellow

FOUR TIMES RUNNER-UP IN THE SUNTORY WORLD MATCH-PLAY, SANDY LYLE WAS DUE A VICTORY WHEN HE REACHED HIS FIFTH FINAL. FACING HIM WAS NICK FALDO, MAKING HIS SECOND APPEARANCE IN A FINAL, AND BETWEEN THEM THEY PRODUCED ANOTHER MEMORABLE CONTEST ROUND WENTWORTH'S BURMA ROAD.

seeds, Ballesteros and Woosnam were first and second favourites respectively but although Europe had an unprecedented four seeds, they all had to deal with some sticky opponents once the first round matches had been concluded.

These games pitted US PGA champion Jeff Sluman against Japan's Nobuo Serizawa; the leading US Tour money-winner, Joey Sindelar, against Britain's Barry Lane; Open Championship runner-up Nick Price against Australia's Rodger Davis and US Tournament Players' champion Mark McCumber against Zimbabwe's Mark McNulty.

Torrential rain on the first morning

caused a suspension of play for a couple of hours and memories of last year's hurricane were recalled. In the top match, Sluman always had the edge on Serizawa and when he won three of the last four holes in the morning to lunch four up the outcome was never in doubt.

As the only British player in action on the first day, Lane took the bulk of the crowd with him but sadly he provided little for them to cheer. He lost two of the first three holes to par figures and was clearly nervous, leaving Sindelar to go round in 69 in the morning, four up. The first hole in the afternoon saw Lane miss a short putt to win the hole and for the next three holes it was all downhill for the Scottish Open winner. He lost the lot and was seven down and thinking of a 10 & 8 margin. Sindelar may have mentally relaxed for Lane then won the fifth and sixth in par and then turning for home, picked up the 10th and 11th to come back to just three down. Sindelar woke up to the dangers and stopped the flow with a birdie at the 12th where Lane's two-iron second shot missed the green and flew into a spectator's coat. A free drop followed but Lane was unable to get down in two more and that was the end of his fight-back.

Price produced the best golf of the morning, round in 68 and four up on Davis. The Australian is a gritty competitor and hung on grimly before a relieved Price finally closed out his man on the 35th.

The McCumber/McNulty match was another stern contest in which fortunes fluctuated. McCumber was two down after six holes but, with four birdies in the last five holes, turned that deficit into a three-hole advantage at lunch. McNulty came back and by the 14th had taken a one-hole lead. A fatal error on the 15th where he took five allowed McCumber's par to square matters and when the American finished with three successive birdies to McNulty's two, the battle of the Macs was concluded.

Undoubtedly the match of the quarter-finals was the one between McCumber and the Big Mac himself, Ballesteros. On a wild, blustery day it seemed likely that McCumber, who hits his shots in a left to right fading pattern, would be outgunned by the longer-hitting Open champion. Ballesteros won the first hole in par but from there on was struggling. McCumber, one up at the turn, won the 10th with a birdie and then played the last four holes in level fours to pick up two more and finish the morning four up. Ballesteros had to strike early if he was going to get back into the match and he did when he struck two imperious blows into the first to win the hole. But he was still struggling and three down after 27.

It was then that McCumber began to realise the enormity of what he might be doing and began an extravagant run of mediocrity over the homeward nine. The vital hole was the 16th where Ballesteros hooked into trees and was still short of the green in three. McCumber left his approach well short and then three-putted to only halve a hole he clearly should have won. Two more halves followed and so the pair trudged off down the 37th. Two stunning wood shots to 12 feet and the putt holed gave Ballesteros a win that even he admitted owed more to McCumber's faltering than any good play on his part.

If that match contained the true elements of match-play cut and thrust, the clash between Lyle and Price provided yet another chapter of disbelief in the event's history. Price was again solid as a rock in the morning and round in 68 to lunch two up. Lyle then began his afternoon round with three consecutive fives – two bogeys and one double-bogey – and was quickly five down. It was what he needed to wake him up. From then on his golf was spectacular and Price's game began to crumble. Lyle was five under par for the last 15 holes and had performed another historic escape.

The Woosnam/Sluman encounter was hard fought for the first nine holes but the defending champion began to pull away as Sluman struggled in the conditions. Round in 69 in the morning, Woosnam was three up and at five under par for 30 holes sent his man packing by the old dog licence.

McNulty succumbed to ...

... McCumber in the battle of the Marks

Extension through the ball from Joey Sindelar

*Japan's Nobuo
Serizawa*

*Jeff Sluman was no
match for Ian Woosnam*

*Barry Lane was down
the road after one round*

Faldo was remorseless against Sindelar. He was three up after 18 then began the afternoon round by chipping in for a birdie at the first and followed that with an eagle at the fourth. Sindelar was half the man he had been against Lane and his driving had deserted him. He came back to three down after 27 holes but Faldo put him away with a run of solid pars from the turn to earn a semi-final spot against Woosnam.

The two Ryder Cup partners were meeting for the first time in the Championship and Woosnam was keeping his nose just ahead. He was not behind until the 31st and then Faldo's unrelenting accuracy gave no quarter. A birdie at the 35th put Faldo ahead and he hung on for a place in the final.

The other semi-final between Lyle and Ballesteros produced golf of staggering quality, with most of it flowing from the clubs of Lyle. Ballesteros was pulling against a tight rein and looked tired, as well he might after such a superlative season. Nonetheless he was round a long and wet course in 67 in the morning, only to find himself two down to Lyle's 64 which was completed with an eagle on the 18th. Ballesteros went tamely after lunch, losing two of the first three holes to pars and then Lyle turned it on again. A holed second shot to the sixth put him virtually out of reach and when he finally shook hands with Ballesteros on the 30th green he was 13 under par for the day, phenomenal golf in the conditions.

So the match to decide the club championship of Wentworth was all set for its usual Sunday conclusion. But yet again, as at the Open Championship, the weather was to have the final say. It rained solidly until 3pm by which time the course was unplayable and a Monday finish had to be arranged.

On a lovely, crisp autumn day Lyle and Faldo set off in cagey fashion, exchanged four holes in the first nine holes and were all square. They remained that way after 14 holes, sharing the short 14th in birdies. Then Lyle struck. He saved a half at the 15th with a brave putt, birdied from 15 feet on the 16th, struck two massive blows onto the 17th green and then holed from fully 30 feet for an eagle. His play of the 18th would have broken most men. A hooked drive from the tee, a hack out up the fairway, a pulled approach and then a chip into the hole for an outrageous birdie. Faldo, who had played the hole immaculately, suddenly found himself having to hole a nasty putt of four feet to save the half. He made it but was two down to Lyle's round of 66.

*Reflections on a
rain-sodden championship*

Double rainbow for
Rodger Davis on the 10th tee

Faldo had to get back into the match quickly after lunch and he did, winning the second and third to square the match. Still all square after 27 holes, Faldo got his nose in front for the first time when Lyle three-putted the 10th. Back came Lyle at the next to square but he was behind again after 12 and then missed an easy winning putt at the 13th. At the short 14th, the 32nd of the match, Faldo's tee shot finished just 10 feet away, Lyle's a distant 30. But it was Lyle who holed and Faldo who missed in the classic match-play swing.

Lyle then struck a superb four iron to within three feet of the hole at the 15th to go one up, matched Faldo's birdie on the 16th and was in the driver's seat on the 17th having finished on the front edge of the green in two. From there he putted right across the green to join Faldo on the back fringe in three strokes. Faldo couldn't hole his attempt but Lyle's putt was straight and true into the back of the hole to give him a victory he richly deserved.

It was Lyle's ability to switch his game into another gear that was the key to his victory. He did it against Price and Ballesteros and again in the final. His play of the inward holes from the 14th in both morning and afternoon was quite remarkable, covering the nine holes they comprised in nine under par. He finished the week 25 under par for all his matches, not the record, which stands at 32 under by Woosnam last year, but still an impressive haul over the 99 holes he played.

The first prize of £75,000 tacked onto his wins in the Dunhill British Masters, US Masters, Greensboro and Phoenix made him the first player this year to pass one million dollars in prize-money but the Suntory title is one he has long sought and its capture will add shine to a record that is already among the proudest of modern times.

Nick Price putts for the end
of the rainbow at the ninth

First tee frolics from the semi-finalists:
Ballesteros and Lyle, Woosnam and Faldo ham it up

Mark McCumber's putt to
beat Ballesteros on the 36th green just slides by

FIRST ROUND: OCTOBER 6

WINNER	CTRY	LOSER	CTRY	SCORE	PRIZE MONEY
Jeff SLUMAN	USA	Nobuo SERIZAWA	Jap	6 & 5	First
Joey SINDELAR	USA	Barry LANE	Eng	5 & 4	Round
Nick PRICE	Zim	Rodger DAVIS	Aus	2 & 1	Losers won
Mark McCUMBER	USA	Mark McNULTY	Zim	1 Hole	£10,000

SECOND ROUND: OCTOBER 7

Ian WOOSNAM	Wal	Jeff SLUMAN	USA	7 & 6	Second
Nick FALDO	Eng	Joey SINDELAR	USA	5 & 4	Round
Sandy LYLE	Scot	Nick PRICE	Zim	3 & 2	Losers won
Seve BALLESTEROS	Sp	Mark McCUMBER	USA	at 37th	£15,000

SEMI-FINAL: OCTOBER 8

Sandy LYLE	Scot	Seve BALLESTEROS	Sp	7 & 6	
Nick FALDO	Eng	Ian WOOSNAM	Wal	1 Hole	

PLAY-OFF FOR 3RD & 4TH PLACES

(Play was abandoned on October 9, the play-off was cancelled and the players shared the prize money)

Seve BALLESTEROS	Sp	Ian WOOSNAM	Wal
(£25,000)		(£25,000)	

FINAL: OCTOBER 10

Sandy LYLE	Scot	Nick FALDO	Eng	2 & 1
(£75,000)		(£40,000)		

TOTAL PRIZE MONEY = £265,000

Greenside recovery from the
new champion

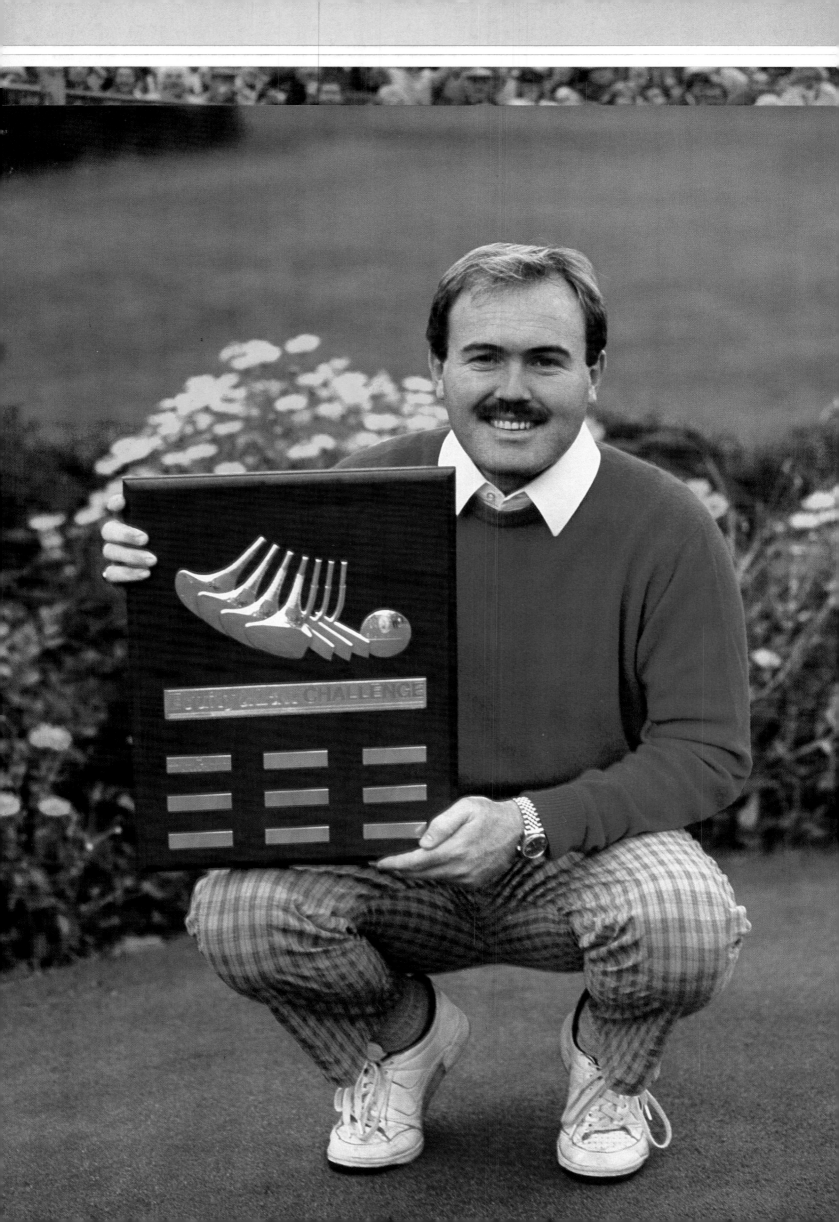

RAFFERTY
takes up the challenge

f unny stuff, money. When you haven't got any it's impossible to find anyone to lend you some. On the other hand, when you've got more than you could reasonably handle, people are falling over themselves to provide you with wads of it.

Following Ireland's victory in the Dunhill Cup, Ronan Rafferty and his team-mates, Eamonn Darcy and Des Smyth, won 100,000 dollars each which worked out at £57,339 per man. The physical and emotional strain of that tumultuous week had left Rafferty exhausted and he had decided that he would withdraw from the Equity & Law Challenge which was to begin at Royal Mid-Surrey on the Monday after the Dunhill Cup. When he telephoned the sponsors to inform them, he was told that if he played there would be a £1,000 bonus for him on top of any prize-money he might win.

The Rafferty bonus came about because Gordon Brand Junior, who had finished fourth in the season-long Equity & Law points system table, had decided not to play and forfeited his £1,000 bonus thereby allowing Rafferty, who finished fifth, to move up a spot and claim it if he wished. He did wish and it turned out to be a very shrewd decision.

The Equity & Law Challenge is a unique competition run in conjunction with the 26 Volvo Tour events that are staged up to September 26th. Throughout those 26 tournaments, a tally of birdies, eagles and albatrosses is kept on each player with one point being awarded for a birdie, two for an eagle and three for an albatross. The leading 30 points winners go forward for a final shoot-out over 54 holes. The leading four players in the points table each receive a bonus which they can only collect if they play at Royal Mid-Surrey.

EXHAUSTED BY HIS EFFORTS ON BEHALF OF IRELAND THE PREVIOUS WEEK, RONAN RAFFERTY STILL FOUND ENOUGH ENERGY TO TAKE HIS FIRST PROFESSIONAL TITLE ON EUROPEAN SOIL.

Richard Boxall, with a total of 341 points, headed the table and won £10,000. Jose-Maria Olazabal was second with 330 points to win £6,000, Eamonn Darcy third with 320 points for £3,000 and Brand Junior fourth with 318 points for £1,000 which ultimately went to Rafferty who was fifth with 314.

This points system makes for attacking golf since there are no deductions for any strokes dropped to par and it is obviously to the liking of Barry Lane. Winner of the inaugural event in 1987, Lane used that maiden European victory as a springboard to greater things and began his defence of the title in no uncertain fashion. To be absolutely truthful, his defence didn't begin until his second nine holes for his first half yielded a measly helping of just one point. From the 10th however, Lane gorged himself. He went birdie, eagle, birdie, eagle – the first eagle coming at the 317-yard 11th when he holed out from a bunker and the second eagle at the 13th when he drove 264 yards five

inches on this 265 yards hole. Two more birdies gave Lane eight points for the nine holes, a total of nine for the round.

Much consultation followed as to whether the 26 strokes constituted a new world record for nine holes but PGA European Tour officials finally ruled that it did not since the tournament is not played under genuine stroke-play conditions. Snapping at Lane's heels was Carl Mason with eight points, Mark Roe with seven and a host of players, including Rafferty, with six.

The final day began spectacularly when Boxall demonstrated some of the form that headed the points table by holing in one at the 220-yards first with a one iron. It was worth two points but failed to inspire him. The morning running was taken up by Mason and Roe who went into lunch tied on 14 points. Lane had an indifferent round, gleaning just four points, while Rafferty moved well contention with a seven point round to lie one point off the pace.

The final round saw several challengers make a bid for the title. Argentina's Eduardo Romero, who had played so well in the Open Championship, set the target with a concluding seven points for a total of 19. This was matched by Denis Durnian a little later.

Eventually it was Rafferty who made the decisive thrust. Three birdies and an eagle on the homeward run saw him round in 60 over the 5,802-yards course, worth eight points for a total of 21.

The victory was Rafferty's first in Europe although he has won in Australia and Venezuela. The £20,000 first prize added to his winnings from the Dunhill Cup made it a particularly lucrative three days for the 24-year old Ulsterman. Not forgetting, of course, the additional £1,000 bonus which persuaded him to play in the first place.

ing professional Mark Thomas, now the

ments that Thomas had recommended.

of four-balls starting at the second, the

F A L D O ' S

fitting finale

When Sandy Lyle arrived at Sotogrande's second course, the one we always used to know as Las Aves, which means the birds in Spanish, but is now known as Valderrama, which apparently doesn't mean anything, he liked what he saw. He noted that the thick, coarse grass around the greens reminded him of the collar of rough that nearly always frames the greens at a US Open. He walked on the manicured fairways and thought to himself that he hadn't seen such texture from tee to green on any golf course other than Augusta National.

When he hit a few putts and discovered that the pace of the undulating greens approached that of the fastest greens on the US Tour, he began to rub his hands in anticipation. 'I, Nick Faldo or Seve will win this tournament' he told his caddie Dave Musgrove. 'They've set it up like an American course and we're the ones most experienced at playing in America.'

And not only set it up. The entire event, from title to tee, was modelled on Augusta. Not for nothing was it called the Volvo Masters and not for nothing was it played on the best-prepared course the pros had seen all season, with an apparently unlimited budget. Each and all of these brought vivid reminders of that other event in April.

Lyle's was an unadventurous choice. As the three best players in the world, one of them was likely to win the Volvo Masters, the last event of the European season, even though a further 70 of the best golfers in Europe would be doing their best to stop them.

In time, Lyle's words were proved prophetically accurate. The tournament at one stage resembled a two-horse race between the reigning US Masters

AFTER A FRUSTRATING SEASON OF RUNNER-UP FINISHES, NICK FALDO WOUND UP THE 1988 VOLVO TOUR WITH A WELL DESERVED VICTORY.

champion and the Open champion. But it was eventually won by Faldo, the man who had come second eight times already in the season and who was playing in his final event anywhere in the world in 1988.

Had he thought about it carefully we ought to have guessed that Faldo might snatch it because both Lyle and Ballesteros had arrived in southern Spain marginally less well-prepared than they might have liked. Lyle was tired and disorientated. The previous week he had made a one-tournament jaunt to Japan followed by recording a film the day after the tournament concluded, which, in turn, was followed by one of those crushingly long flights that start on one continent one day and end on another continent another day – or is it two days? – later. When he got to Sotogrande late on Tuesday evening, he could have been excused for asking what time it was, what day it was and where exactly was he?

Ballesteros may have gone one tournament too far. He didn't commit himself to appearing at Valderrama until the last minute, which suggests that

a part of his mind was on other matters, perhaps on his imminent marriage to his longtime girlfriend Carmen Botin.

Faldo, though, was rested and clear-minded after arriving a few days early to practise and recuperate in the pale sunshine. He was in his element on a course that required patience, nerve and skill, a course where he had made a video with David Leadbetter, the famous coach, earlier in the summer. Weren't these qualities, as well as a transparent unflappability, the very ones he had shown in May 1987 to win the Spanish Open at Las Brisas, which means the breezes, a course that had put the wind up most of his colleagues?

At the start, no-one gave Faldo a second glance. All eyes were on Ballesteros and Lyle. They each had 68s. Faldo had a 74. Almost all the rest were struggling with Robert Trent Jones' awesomely defended course with its tricky greens, three of which had thatch on them, stands of cork oak trees and a tugging Levante wind. Only four men beat par on the opening day – Lyle and Ballesteros and Roger Chapman and Ove Sellberg – and that meant that 74 missed it.

By the second day, matters had become even more bizarre. The grass around the greens was said to be the main culprit. 'I missed three greens today and I took three bogies' said Ballesteros after his second day's 72. 'The grass around the greens is very difficult' he said. 'I don't think Mr Patino wants too many under par.'

In that case Senor Jaime Ortiz-Patino, one of the world's richest men and the owner of the course, got his wish. Lyle's five under par halfway total led Ballesteros by one stroke. The cut was 154 or ten over par, by four shots the highest of the year in Europe. The field was a cumulative 670 over par.

By the end of the third day it was all falling into place. Ballesteros and Lyle had made heavy weather of it on the calmest day of the week. Playing together they had only two birdies between them (both falling to Seve) and their totals were 74 and 75 respectively. Roger Chapman, after hours on the practice ground under the watchful eye of Bob Torrance, had a 70 and was only four behind. Ian Woosnam (70) was five behind, as was Jose-Maria Canizares after the day's best score, a 67.

When he turned in his card, Canizares found his was only the fourth sub-70 round of the event and he had compiled it, moreover, without a single bogey. This may have been a greater achievement than scoring five under par because the course was so unforgiving. Almost every shot on almost every hole was fraught with danger and there simply wasn't a single place where a player could relax. Jose Rivero found this out to his cost when he started out his second round with a run of birdie, bogey, bogey, double-bogey, birdie, bogey, bogey.

But Faldo had ground out a 68. His wedge play had been razor sharp, his putting sound. He moved to within two strokes of Ballesteros and Lyle and now the event had become a three-horse race.

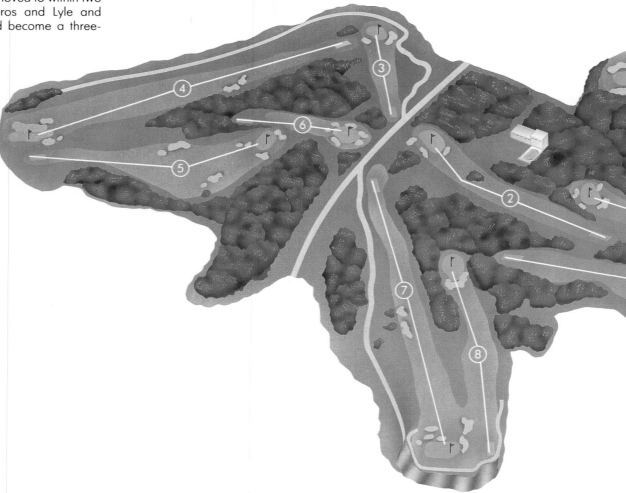

As he began the last round, Faldo felt reassured by words of encouragement Geoff Boycott had given him at the Dunhill Cup. Take no notice of anyone else' the former England cricketer had said. 'You know what is best for you.' By the turn Faldo had drawn level. He had chipped in on the fifth and holed from the fringe on the eighth. On the inward half Faldo turned the screws on his opponents, holing putts of ten feet on the 13th and eight feet at the 16th, putts on the distance that he has often missed this season. That gave him a two-stroke cushion.

Lyle was out of it after another birdie-less round but Ballesteros had one last chance to catch Faldo. A birdie on the 17th would have pressurised the Englishman who was at that moment stymied by a cork oak tree on the 18th. Surprisingly, though, Ballesteros missed from three feet. Faldo, having heard the gasp from the crowd behind, bent his second shot around the tree and into a bunker and from there got up and down for his par. Victory was his by two strokes.

He and Ballesteros were the only two players to finish under par. Seve's second place was worth £38,860 plus £50,000 for winning the Volvo Order of Merit. Faldo took home nearly £60,000 which was sufficient for him to regain second place in the money list.

The win was more important than the money. 'I'd have been bitterly

VALDERRAMA
· GOLF CLUB ·

Hole	Par	Metres	Hole	Par	Metres
1	4	354	10	4	369
2	4	375	11	5	504
3	3	156	12	3	200
4	5	515	13	4	367
5	4	344	14	4	337
6	3	150	15	3	207
7	5	486	16	4	385
8	4	319	17	5	519
9	4	415	18	4	417
OUT	36	3114	IN	36	3305
			TOTAL	72	6419

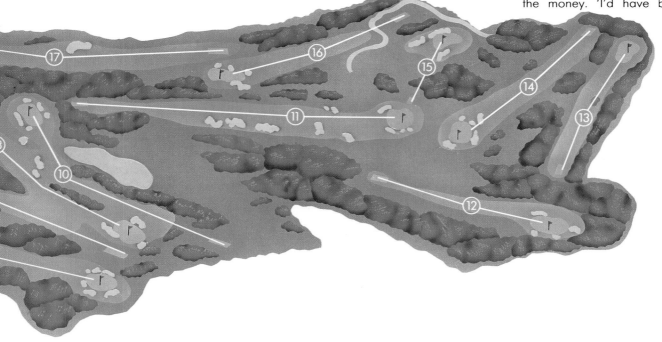

disappointed to have played so well from tee to green and only won the French Open' Faldo said later, reflecting on his eight second place finishes all season, including the US Open and the Suntory World Match-Play. 'Without victory here, I wouldn't have achieved enough this year in my mind. In this game you don't know how long your ability will last so you must win while you're playing well.' At Valderrama, at long last, he did just that.

Ballesteros and Lyle continue to make banner headlines

Course architect Robert Trent Jones, in buggy, and course owner, Jaime Ortiz-Patino, with binoculars, survey the scene

Faldo silhouette

*Rivero takes a hazardous
route on the second*

Barry Lane up a cork tree

*Sandy Lyle weighed down
by another missed putt*

Nick Faldo plays his penultimate shot on the 18th green

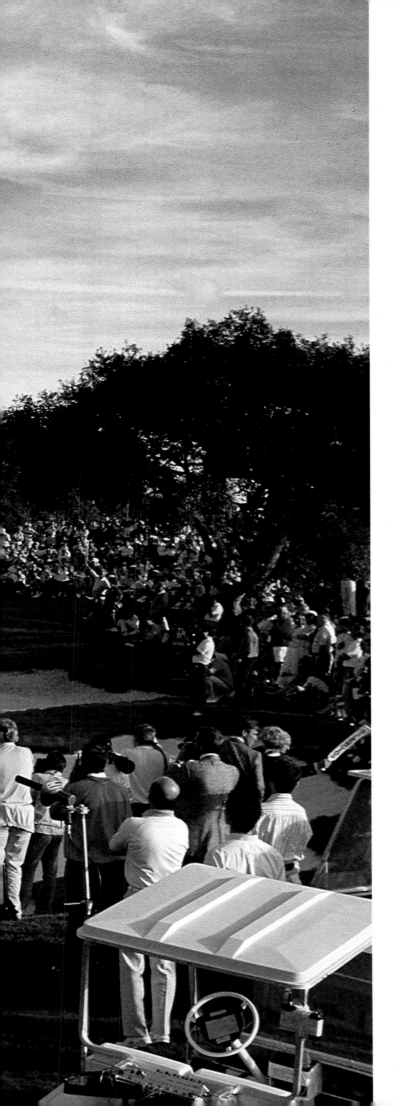

POS	NAME	CTRY	1	2	3	4	TOTAL	PRIZE MONEY
1	Nick FALDO	Eng	74	71	71	68	284	£58330
2	Seve BALLESTEROS	Sp	68	77	74	72	286	£38860
3	Sandy LYLE	Scot	68	71	75	74	288	£21910
4	Ian WOOSNAM	Wal	75	74	70	70	289	£17500
5	Roger CHAPMAN	Eng	71	77	70	75	293	£13540
	Eamonn DARCY	Ire	74	71	74	74	293	£13540
7	Mats LANNER	Swe	77	70	74	73	294	£8522
	Anders SORENSEN	Den	76	67	76	75	294	£8522
	Peter FOWLER	Aus	77	71	71	75	294	£8522
	Christy O'CONNOR Jr	Ire	78	73	70	73	294	£8522
11	Jose Maria CANIZARES	Sp	76	76	67	76	295	£6230
	Neil HANSEN	Eng	77	72	75	71	295	£6230
13	Howard CLARK	Eng	73	73	74	76	296	£5490
	Manuel PINERO	Sp	74	71	81	70	296	£5490
15	Neil COLES	Eng	78	76	72	71	297	£5140
16	Peter BAKER	Eng	72	74	75	77	298	£4628
	Manuel CALERO	Sp	77	73	73	75	298	£4628
	Ove SELLBERG	Swe	71	74	76	77	298	£4628
	Jose Maria OLAZABAL	Sp	78	74	69	77	298	£4628
20	Simon BISHOP	Eng	74	72	79	74	299	£4095
	Tony CHARNLEY	Eng	74	72	75	78	299	£4095
	Des SMYTH	Ire	73	81	71	74	299	£4095
23	David J RUSSELL	Eng	74	79	74	73	300	£3780
	Carl MASON	Eng	75	72	79	74	300	£3780
	Barry LANE	Eng	74	75	75	76	300	£3780
26	Michael ALLEN	USA	73	76	76	76	301	£3206
	David WHELAN	Eng	76	74	77	74	301	£3206
	Mark JAMES	Eng	73	76	76	77	301	£3206
	Ronan RAFFERTY	N.Ire	77	76	71	77	301	£3206
	Vicente FERNANDEZ	Arg	78	76	76	71	301	£3206
	Derrick COOPER	Eng	74	76	73	78	301	£3206
	Gordon J BRAND	Eng	78	76	71	76	301	£3206
	David GILFORD	Eng	77	76	74	74	301	£3206
34	Denis DURNIAN	Eng	73	75	75	79	302	£2730
	Mark MCNULTY	Zim	76	79	71	77	302	£2730
	Eduardo ROMERO	Arg	79	70	77	76	302	£2730
37	Ignacio GERVAS	Sp	82	71	79	71	303	£2485
	David WILLIAMS	Eng	74	76	76	77	303	£2485
	Richard BOXALL	Eng	78	72	79	74	303	£2485
	Paul WAY	Eng	74	78	76	75	303	£2485
41	Ross MCFARLANE	Eng	79	73	80	73	305	£2170
	Johan RYSTROM	Swe	75	77	78	75	305	£2170
	Malcolm MACKENZIE	Eng	73	80	75	77	305	£2170
	Bernard GALLACHER	Scot	76	72	84	73	305	£2170
	Jimmy HEGGARTY	N.Ire	77	76	75	77	305	£2170
46	Bill LONGMUIR	Scot	75	76	83	72	306	£1925
	Paul CURRY	Eng	79	71	78	78	306	£1925
48	Juan ANGLADA	Sp	75	77	76	79	307	£1785
	David FEHERTY	N.Ire	77	77	72	81	307	£1785
50	David LLEWELLYN	Wal	73	76	78	81	308	£1680
51	Sam TORRANCE	Scot	72	81	78	78	309	£1575
	John SLAUGHTER	USA	76	78	76	79	309	£1575

VOLVO ORDER OF MERIT

① Severiano **BALLESTEROS**

Spain

PRIZE MONEY
£451,559.59

② Nick **FALDO**

England

PRIZE MONEY
£347,971.47

③ Jose-Maria **OLAZABAL**

Spain

PRIZE MONEY
£285,964.33

④ Ian **WOOSNAM**

Wales

PRIZE MONEY
£234,990.64

⑤ Sandy **LYLE**

Scotland

PRIZE MONEY
£186,017.98

⑥ Mark **MCNULTY**

Zimbabwe

PRIZE MONEY
£180,991.55

⑦ Des **SMYTH**

Ireland

PRIZE MONEY
£171,951.02

⑧ Mark **JAMES**

England

PRIZE MONEY
£152,900.37

⑨ Ronan **RAFFERTY**

Northern Ireland

PRIZE MONEY
£132,394.66

⑩ Jose **RIVERO**

Spain

PRIZE MONEY
£131,079.42

POS	NAME	CTRY	PRIZE MONEY
11	Gordon BRAND Jr	Scot	£129296.79
12	Peter BAKER	Eng	£125182.08
13	Howard CLARK	Eng	£124373.64
14	Barry LANE	Eng	£119209.83
15	Eamonn DARCY	Ire	£112335.22
16	Peter SENIOR	Aus	£103101.47
17	Roger CHAPMAN	Eng	£99758.15
18	Mark MOULAND	Wal	£95580.95
19	Chris MOODY	Eng	£95567.27
20	Denis DURNIAN	Eng	£94909.32
21	Rodger DAVIS	Aus	£93203.49
22	Anders FORSBRAND	Swe	£89880.90
23	Christy O'CONNOR Jr	Ire	£84456.52
24	Craig PARRY	Aus	£81782.54
25	Miguel MARTIN	Sp	£76184.19
26	Carl MASON	Eng	£75887.22
27	Richard BOXALL	Eng	£72392.80
28	Gordon J BRAND	Eng	£69908.20
29	Mike HARWOOD	Aus	£68843.27
30	Bernhard LANGER	W.Ger	£66368.38
31	Philip WALTON	Ire	£66155.98
32	Derek COOPER	Eng	£65101.68
33	Frank NOBILO	NZ	£64706.19
34	Wayne RILEY	Aus	£63782.92
35	Manuel PINERO	Sp	£63006.12
36	Peter FOWLER	Aus	£59521.61
37	José Maria CANIZARES	Sp	£54474.75
38	Tony JOHNSTONE	Zim	£53792.85
39	Tony CHARNLEY	Eng	£51604.31
40	David WHELAN	Eng	£51450.83
41	Jeff HAWKES	SA	£51034.93
42	David J RUSSELL	Eng	£50782.40
43	David WILLIAMS	Eng	£48580.03
44	Mats LANNER	Swe	£43533.75
45	David FEHERTY	N.Ire	£43346.29
46	Mark ROE	Eng	£42835.37
47	Mike SMITH	USA	£42828.55
48	Eduardo ROMERO	Arg	£42752.93
49	David LLEWELLYN	Wal	£42680.30
50	Andrew MURRAY	Eng	£42252.11
51	Sam TORRANCE	Scot	£42251.69
52	Colin MONTGOMERIE	Scot	£39201.42
53	Mike CLAYTON	Aus	£39041.01
54	Michael ALLEN	USA	£37351.07
55	Stephen BENNETT	Eng	£37162.23
56	John MORGAN	Eng	£36262.84
57	Ove SELLBERG	Swe	£35964.76
58	Jim RUTLEDGE	Can	£34507.49
59	Malcolm MACKENZIE	Eng	£34313.20
60	Bill LONGMUIR	Scot	£34029.34
61	John BLAND	SA	£33888.63
62	Ian MOSEY	Eng	£33576.75
63	Andrew SHERBORNE	Eng	£33288.29
64	Jerry ANDERSON	Can	£33195.36
65	Gerry TAYLOR	Aus	£31542.50
66	Magnus PERSSON	Swe	£30957.60
67	David GILFORD	Eng	£30626.07
68	Hugh BAIOCCHI	SA	£29781.23
69	Ossie MOORE	Aus	£29208.23
70	Philip HARRISON	Eng	£29088.00
71	Brett OGLE	Aus	£28936.93
72	Neil HANSEN	Eng	£28716.96
73	Ron COMMANS	USA	£27995.81
74	Manuel CALERO	Sp	£27565.99
75	Martin POXON	Eng	£26852.58
76	Peter MITCHELL	Eng	£26623.93

POS	NAME	CTRY	PRIZE MONEY
77	Brian MARCHBANK	Scot	£26174.21
78	Anders SORENSEN	Den	£26016.22
79	Johan RYSTROM	Swe	£25605.20
80	Bob SHEARER	Aus	£25331.01
81	John SLAUGHTER	USA	£25181.43
82	David A RUSSELL	Eng	£25165.56
83	Juan ANGLADA	Sp	£25161.83
84	Antonio GARRIDO	Sp	£24374.85
85	Paul CURRY	Eng	£24243.14
86	David RAY	Eng	£23238.15
87	Glenn RALPH	Eng	£22721.78
88	Emmanuel DUSSART	Fr	£20987.16
89	Vicente FERNANDEZ	Arg	£20653.08
90	Peter MCWHINNEY	Aus	£20579.56
91	John JACOBS	USA	£20438.26
92	Jimmy HEGGARTY	N.Ire	£20266.23
93	Ignacio GERVAS	Sp	£19812.13
94	Paul WAY	Eng	£19736.56
95	Ross MCFARLANE	Eng	£19715.90
96	Simon BISHOP	Eng	£19656.92
97	Bob E SMITH	USA	£18560.17
98	Ken BROWN	Scot	£18112.46
99	Bernard GALLACHER	Scot	£18017.63
100	Peter TERAVAINEN	USA	£17774.74
101	Lyndsay STEPHEN	Aus	£17388.80
102	Andrew OLDCORN	Eng	£16704.39
103	Jerry HAAS	USA	£16242.01
104	Bill MALLEY	USA	£15820.53
105	Paul KENT	Eng	£15522.62
106	Emilio RODRIGUEZ	Sp	£14936.14
107	Stephen MCALLISTER	Scot	£14714.16
108	Keith WATERS	Eng	£14650.48
109	Ian YOUNG	Scot	£14152.35
110	Armando SAAVEDRA	Arg	£14055.11
111	Gavin LEVENSON	SA	£13942.22
112	Ross DRUMMOND	Scot	£13871.54
113	Mats HALLBERG	Swe	£13867.08
114	Michael KING	Eng	£13673.64
115	Grant TURNER	Eng	£13488.95
116	Philip PARKIN	Wal	£13428.82
117	Noel RATCLIFFE	Aus	£13326.06
118	Bryan NORTON	USA	£13279.13
119	Marc PENDARIES	Fr	£13195.31
120	Steen TINNING	Den	£13120.79
121	Robert LEE	Eng	£12902.09
122	Magnus SUNESSON	Swe	£12876.92
123	Andrew CHANDLER	Eng	£12681.81
124	Kyi Hla HAN	Bur	£12502.31
125	John DE FOREST	USA	£11941.14
126	David JONES	N.Ire	£11922.05
127	Frederic REGARD	Fr	£11587.02
128	Alberto BINAGHI	It	£11580.81
129	Mitch ADCOCK	USA	£11405.70
130	Teddy WEBBER	Zim	£11299.81
131	Luis CARBONETTI	Arg	£9594.81
132	Santiago LUNA	Sp	£9587.75
133	Wayne SMITH	Aus	£9078.71
134	Vaughan SOMERS	Aus	£8892.90
135	Bill MCCOLL	Scot	£8221.20
136	Craig MCCLELLAN	USA	£8114.05
137	Peter JONES	Aus	£8036.11
138	John MCHENRY	Ire	£7773.23
139	Paul THOMAS	Wal	£7697.84
140	Mike MILLER	Scot	£7649.85
141	Russell WEIR	Scot	£7458.21
142	Magnus JONSSON	Swe	£7435.11

POS	NAME	CTRY	PRIZE MONEY
143	Neal BRIGGS	Eng	£7310.68
144	Ronald STELTEN	USA	£6661.90
145	Jesper PARNEVIK	Swe	£6589.32
146	Rick HARTMANN	USA	£6385.45
147	Jamie HOWELL	USA	£6278.71
148	Martin SLUDDS	Ire	£6102.82
149	Emanuele BOLOGNESI	It	£5437.58
150	Mark DAVIS	Eng	£5079.14
151	Jeremy BENNETT	Eng	£4977.87
152	Tony STEVENS	Eng	£4922.49
153	Jeff HALL	Eng	£4629.35
154	Steven BOTTOMLEY	Eng	£4333.86
155	Mikael KARLSSON	Swe	£3964.02
156	Mariano APARICIO	Sp	£3943.00
157	Greg J TURNER	NZ	£3663.33
158	Michael MCLEAN	Eng	£3401.92
159	Joe HIGGINS	Eng	£3186.55
160	Ian ROBERTS	Aus	£3051.55
161	John O'LEARY	Ire	£2936.33
162	Gary WEBB	USA	£2852.11
163	Carlo KNAUSS	W.Ger	£2756.29
164	Michel TAPIA	Fr	£2641.85
165	Clive TUCKER	Eng	£2604.00
166	Gery WATINE	Fr	£2501.19
167	Miguel JIMENEZ	Sp	£2496.40
168	Marc Antoine FARRY	Fr	£2437.41
169	Wayne STEPHENS	Eng	£2429.97
170	Andrew STUBBS	Eng	£2272.71
171	Simon TOWNEND	Eng	£2207.87
172	Magnus GRANKVIST	Swe	£2188.17
173	Craig LAURENCE	Eng	£2060.76
174	David R JONES	Eng	£1975.00
175	Oliver ECKSTEIN	W.Ger	£1899.18
176	Carl Magnus STROEMBERG	Swe	£1896.71
177	Jose DAVILA	Sp	£1809.74
178	Mark LITTON	Wal	£1800.39
179	Peter DAHLBERG	Swe	£1789.02
180	Brian WATTS	USA	£1785.55
181	Paul CARRIGILL	Eng	£1610.12
182	Bryan LEWIS	Scot	£1600.76
183	Daniel WESTERMARK	Swe	£1542.00
184	Jeremy ROBINSON	Eng	£1470.97
185	Jacob RASMUSSEN	Den	£1280.00
186	Glyn DAVIES	Wal	£1239.50
187	Clas HULTMAN	Swe	£1113.17
	John HAWKSWORTH	Eng	£1113.17
189	Richard FISH	Eng	£1084.00
190	Bobby MITCHELL	Eng	£1060.00
191	Alessandro ROGATO	It	£954.00
192	Wraith GRANT	Eng	£945.38
193	Paul MAYO	Wal	£932.50
194	Stephen HAMILL	N.Ire	£832.00
195	Chip DRURY	USA	£775.24
196	Jonas SAXTON	USA	£763.00
197	Andrea CANESSA	It	£742.00
198	Roger MACKAY	Aus	£692.00
199	Andrew COTTON	Eng	£654.00
200	Laurie TURNER	Eng	£580.00
201	David WOOD	Wal	£566.52
202	Philip HINTON	Eng	£520.00
	Paul HOAD	Eng	£520.00
204	Michael FEW	Eng	£482.07
205	Leif HEDERSTROM	Swe	£450.00
	Lindsay MANN	Scot	£450.00
207	Peter CARSBO	Swe	£404.59
208	Ross WHITEHEAD	Eng	£400.00

contributors

Bill Blighton (Today)	–	*The German Masters*
Mike Britten (Exchange Telegraph)	–	*Mallorca Open de Baleares*
	–	*Torras Hostench Barcelona Open*
	–	*AGF Biarritz Open*
	–	*Volvo Cannes Open*
	–	*Cepsa Madrid Open*
	–	*Portuguese Open*
	–	*Peugeot Spanish Open*
	–	*Lancia Italian Open*
	–	*Belgian Volvo Open*
	–	*Peugeot French Open*
	–	*Monte Carlo Golf Open*
	–	*KLM Open*
	–	*Scandinavian Enterprise Open*
	–	*PLM Open*
	–	*BNP Jersey Open*
David Davies (The Guardian)	–	*Volvo Order of Merit Winner*
Richard Dodd (The Yorkshire Post)	–	*English Open*
Alan Fraser (Scotland on Sunday)	–	*Bell's Scottish Open*
Mark Garrod (Press Association)	–	*Wang Four Stars National Pro-Celebrity*
Dermot Gilleece (The Irish Times)	–	*Carrolls Irish Open*
Tim Glover (The Independent)	–	*Ebel European Masters/Swiss Open*
John Hopkins (The Sunday Times)	–	*Epson Grand Prix of Europe*
	–	*Volvo PGA Championship*
	–	*Trophée Lancôme*
	–	*Volvo Masters*
Derek Lawrenson (The Birmingham Post & Mail)	–	*Benson and Hedges International Open*
Norman Mair (The Scotsman)	–	*Dunhill British Masters*
Michael McDonnell (The Daily Mail)	–	*The Year in Retrospect*
Alister Nicol (The Daily Record)	–	*Volvo Seniors British Open*
Marino Parascenzo (The Pittsburgh Post Gazette)	–	*The American Class of '88*
Mitchell Platts (The Times)	–	*German Open*
Chris Plumridge (The Illustrated London News)	–	*117th Open Championship*
	–	*Panasonic European Open*
	–	*Suntory World Match-Play*
	–	*Equity & Law Challenge*
Andrew Totham (Golf World)	–	*The Growth of European Golf*
Michael Williams (The Daily Telegraph)	–	*Dunhill Cup*

VOLVO TOUR YEARBOOK

photographers

Charles Briscoe-Knight — *pages 3, 5 (bottom), 6, 8 (top right, middle four, bottom right), 9 (top, middle bottom, bottom right), 11 (top left & right, bottom right), 13, 14, 15 (right, bottom left & right), 20, 21, 27, 36, 37, 44, 56, 58, 59, 60, 61, 62/63, 64, 65, 66, 67, 68, 69, 74, 75, 82, 83, 84, 85, 97, 98, 99, 101, 102, 106, 107 (top right & bottom), 108, 110, 111, 112, 113, 114, 115, 116/117, 119 (top right & bottom right), 120, 121, 122, 128, 129, 130, 131, 132, 133, 134, 136, 137, 138/139, 142, 146, 164, 165, 166, 167, 168, 169, 170, 171, 173, 176, 177, 178 (middle & right), 179, 180, 181, 188, 189, 190/191, 192, 193, 196 (top), 197, 200, 202, (top far left, left, right & far right), 203, 204, 205, 207, 208, 211, 212 (bottom), 213, 214, 217, 224, 225, 229, 230/231, 232, 233 (top), 236, 238, 239*

Phil Sheldon — *page 7, 9, (middle right), 10, 16, 17, 18, 19, 22, 23, 24, 26, 28, 42, 43, 45, 46, 47, 48, 49, 50, 51, 76, 77, 80 (large), 107 (top centre), 109, 118, 119 (top left), 143, 194, 195, 196 (bottom left & right), 198, 199, 210, 212 (top), 215, 218, 219, 220, 228*

Didier Chicot — *pages 9 (middle top, middle), 15 (top left), 29, 32, 33, 86, 88, 89, 90 (right), 91 (bottom), 92, 93, 94 (bottom), 182, 184 (top right & left), 185, 186, 187*

Lawrence N. Levy — *pages 4 (bottom), 54 (bottom), 55, 80 (insets), 81 (bottom), 178/179, 183, 184 (bottom), 240*

Peter Dazeley — *pages 1, 2, 57, 70 (left), 72/73, 78, 79, 81 (top), 125, 126, 127, 172, 173, 174, 175, 178 (left)*

Mathew Harris — *pages 8 (bottom left), 11 (bottom left), 12, 216, 233 (bottom left & right)*

Ludovic Aubert — *pages 30, 31, 34, 35 (top), 91 (top)*

Claude Granveaud — *pages 35 (bottom), 87, 90 (left), 94 (top)*

Trevor Jones — *pages 134, 135, 140, 141*

M. Nuria Pastor — *pages 38, 95*

ABR — *pages 39, 40, 41*

Olympia — *pages 53, 54 (top), 55*

Margot Briscoe-Knight — *pages 206, 234*

Jan Ebbinge — *pages 123, 124*

Dave Cannon — *pages 201, 202 (bottom)*

Anders Nordlund — *pages 144, 145*

David Ferguson — *pages 222, 223*

Andrew Bailey — *page 221*